Praise for

Theodore Niretac Tinker and
Fiction Tinker's Guide to Whimsical Worlds

Theodore Niretac Tinker has created a handy gem with *Fiction Tinker's Guide to Whimsical Worlds*. From love to nature to language in an author's world, he tackles it all. In this easy-to-digest guide, Tod takes authors on a journey and offers thought-provoking questions and sage recommendations to consider as they craft and refine their own worlds.

—Amy Megill
www.EditorAmy.com

Tod made me feel completely at ease. We delved into character development, and he gave me ideas on how to keep everything in order. How to keep with my timeline and cut out mundane parts. Not once did I feel like I shouldn't even be writing or what am I thinking calling myself an author? He was very encouraging and even gave me ideas for a series! I walked away with the desire to immediately tackle my story and renewed and refreshed perspective to do it! Thank you so much, Tod!

—Carla Davis
Client, TNT Editing

Praise For

As both an editor and author, I plan on returning to *Fiction Tinker's Guide to Whimsical Worlds* over and over again. It has such a fantastic variety of topics and examples one might need to create a well-developed world, whether it's Earth as we know it or an entirely new, magical land. I'm already looking forward to using it for my next series!

—Cait Marie
Author, The Nihryst Series

I struggle so hard when it comes to narrowing down plot while keeping world and character building intact. Tod was genius in not just talking through my story with me and helping me nail down specific plot points but also identifying elements that could be added for a richer story. . . . I'll definitely be back again and again!

—Debbie Burns
Author, *The Path to Courage*

Tod Tinker is a gifted and meticulous editor who spots flaws in a story's logic and has helped me clarify my thinking and intentions for many pieces of writing. Tod is also a coach who pushes me to do my best work by firmly yet gracefully encouraging me to experiment with other approaches or try different ways.

—Dustin Grinnell
Client, TNT Editing

Fiction Tinker's Guide to

Whimsical Worlds

FICTION TINKER'S GUIDE TO

WHIMSICAL WORLDS

21 TIPS FOR DEFINING YOUR WORLD

THEODORE NIRETAC TINKER

BALANCE OF SEVEN

Dallas

For information, contact:
Balance of Seven, www.balanceofseven.com
Publisher: dyfreeman@balanceofseven.com
Managing Editor: tntinker@balanceofseven.com

Illustrations and Cover Design by Holla Watson
Sweet Issues Art, www.sweet-issues-art.com

Developmental Editing by Ynes Freeman, Charleigh Brennan

Copy Editing by Kathy Riggs Larsen

Formatting by TNT Editing, www.theodorentinker.com

Publisher's Cataloging-in-Publication Data
Names: Tinker, Theodore Niretac, author. | Tinker, Dorothy Catherine.
Title: Fiction tinker's guide to whimsical worlds : 21 tips for defining your world / Theodore Niretac Tinker.
Description: Dallas, TX : Balance of Seven, 2021. | Series: Fiction tinker's guide ; 1. | Includes 21 b&w drawings and 2 b&w photos. | Includes bibliographical references and index.
Identifiers: LCCN 2021931431 | ISBN 9781947012110 (pbk.) | ISBN 9781947012127 (ebook)
Subjects: LCSH: Creative writing. | Fantasy literature – Authorship. | Setting (Literature). | BISAC: LANGUAGE ARTS & DISCIPLINES / Writing / Fiction Writing. | LANGUAGE ARTS & DISCIPLINES / Writing / Authorship.
Classification: LCC PN3377.5.F34 T56 2021 (print) | PN3377.5.F34 (ebook) | DDC 808.3876 T56--dc23
LC record available at https://lccn.loc.gov/2021931431

25 24 23 22 21   1 2 3 4 5

CONTENTS

Contents

Introduction

Going on an Adventure

Theodore Niretac Tinker here—spec-fic trans author, meticulous editor, and deep-diving world-builder. Words and worlds are my passion; quality and consistency, my goal. I spend my days diving not only into my own worlds but into those of other writers. With this book, I will guide you through the journey of bringing your own immersive worlds to life.

Exploring Whimsical Worlds

The Fiction Tinker's Guide editing series began as a series of tips posted on my social media under the hashtag #EditingTidbit. Each tidbit covers a different editing topic and is meant to make writers think about their stories and worlds in ways they may not have considered before.

The twenty-one tips presented and discussed in this volume focus on worldbuilding topics that can be applied to the world of any fictional story: historical, modern, or speculative fiction. Most likely, not all topics will feature in each of your stories, but getting to know every portion of your world will help you better portray that world throughout your story.

THE ROAD MAP

This book uses as its road map the acronym PERSIAN: political, economic, religious, social, intellectual, artistic, and natural. Historical and anthropological studies use this acronym to explore the different aspects of a society's culture. I use this acronym when teaching worldbuilding, and it is the pattern I followed to organize the tips in this book.

With one exception: I always begin with the nature of the world.

When it comes to your story, the nature of the world provides the setting, even if the setting is not natural. Nature can be broken into two parts: the lay of the land and the law of the land. The lay of the land is the physical: the maps, the structural design and layout of buildings and ships, the terrain, and the climate. The law of the land is the world's nature beyond the physical and is the topic of the first tip in this book.

The Road Map

N—Nature of the World

P—Political Aspects

E—Economic Aspects

R—Religious Aspects

S—Social Aspects

I—Intellectual Aspects

A—Artistic Aspects

FOLLOWING THE MAP

This book is meant to be used again and again, for building multiple worlds across multiple stories. You can read through it at your leisure and get a sense of the meaning of each tidbit—the signposts along our worldbuilding journey. Once you have gotten a sense of the book, I recommend you choose one of the worlds you are writing, read through the tips again, and consider how each may apply to that particular world and the people within it.

Do this when you are stuck in a story and do not know how to move it forward. Do this when you are creating a new world and diving into each of its aspects. Do this when you are revising a story and trying to make it more real and enticing for your reader.

THE TREASURE WE SEEK

The goal of this adventure is to better understand the worlds you write: how they work, why the people within them act the way they do, and where the characters of your stories fit within them. The twenty-one tidbits are laid out individually, but they frequently interact. As you move through them, you may find they feed into each other.

Also, keep in mind that these tips are written to cover as much breadth for each topic as possible. You will most likely seek more detailed research as each tidbit expands the possibilities for your worlds.

The most important treasure to find in this adventure, however, is the true nature of the world of your story. Do not insert creatures, rituals, customs, and more just for the sake of having them. Instead, let these tidbits guide you deeper into your world. Use them to consider why your world is the way it is and what may be missing based on what you already know and what already exists.

PART I

NATURE OF THE WORLD

Set your world's laws of nature and
stick to them. Your world can break
Earth's natural laws but not its own.

TIDBIT 1

LAW OF THE LAND

**Set your world's laws of nature and
stick to them. Your world can break
Earth's natural laws but not its own.**

Whether you write contemporary fiction or science
fiction / fantasy, the world you write should have
natural laws that remain consistent throughout the
story. If you are writing contemporary fiction, you
may be lucky enough to find them already built for
you in the laws of nature you observe every day. If
you are writing genre fiction, especially in a world that
is decidedly not Earth, you can expand beyond Earth
rules and even reinvent them as you create the world
of your story.

DETERMINING WHAT TO FOCUS ON

If you write contemporary fiction, the laws of nature may not be something you need to worry about. Instead, focus on the cultural or social norms and customs set in place by religions, governments, or economies. Such norms and customs should guide the actions of your characters, even if their actions rebel against them. The norms and customs act as a framework for characters to obey or reject.

For those writing in more "what-if" genres, the natural laws become an important tool. If your writing covers a spiritual topic or the supernatural, the nature of the soul and the presence or absence of deities and similar beings should be mapped out. If you are working on science fiction, you will want to define the laws of physics and how they differ from real-world physics or the technologies used and how they work. For fantasy and paranormal pieces, the existence and definitions of magic are laws unto themselves. The presence of any nonhuman creatures (alien, magical, or otherwise) should fit within whatever natural laws you define.

The above are generalizations more than anything else. Your story may require all three—spiritual, science, and magic—to be defined to varying degrees. It is also possible that different types of people or different regions or worlds within one universe might have dissimilar rules. Fitting them together and creating an overarching set of natural laws that encompasses everything is most important.

DEFINING THE SPIRITUAL

It is important to note that spiritual law is not the same as religious beliefs. As a writer, you understand your story's world in a way that is not possible in real life. You determine which deities exist and what happens on a spiritual plane beyond mortals' full understanding. You define the existence of souls and what occurs to them during mortal life and beyond. You decide how much communication and inter-action occurs between spiritual beings and mortals and how such interaction happens.

If you are uncertain which spiritual laws fit your world best, I recommend researching the spiritual and religious beliefs of yours and other cultures and then making your own for your world. Be mindful, though, of how you use practices that are unfamiliar to you. If you base the spiritual law of your world on an existing religion that is not your own, consider bringing in a sensitivity reader to avoid cultural appropriation or misrepresentation issues.

DEFINING THE SCIENCE

The science side of speculative fiction may be intimidating for some writers to address. More than once, I have heard of writers who delved into science fiction and were chastised for presenting science that did not fit within today's scientific framework. However, science fiction is not about technology being probable based on the science we currently know; it is about technology being feasible based on the scientific laws within a story's world. The technology you create for your story should connect logically to the laws of nature you set in place. It does not matter how your world's technology relates to the natural laws we deal with in real life; however, you may be able to use the similarities and differences between your world and the real world to help your readers understand.

DEFINING THE MAGIC

Some consider magic to be the easiest form of "what if" because so many things can be blamed on magic without requiring a specific cause. However, magic is also the likeliest to be portrayed inconsistently. Without defining and possibly restricting where magic comes from or how it is performed (through wands, staves, rituals, spells, talismans, etc.), a writer can introduce a new form of magic late in the story that either confuses the reader or reads as a deus ex machina (i.e., a contrived solution provided for an insoluble situation).

When discussing different ways magic may work, I like to refer to the various magic classes represented in games like Dungeons and Dragons: sorcerer, wizard, cleric, warlock, druid, and even bard. Generally, each class derives its magic from a different source. Sorcerers pull their magic from an internal source that may be tied to a bloodline. Wizards are scholarly magic wielders, learning their magic through books and spells passed down through the ages. Clerics wield divine magic granted to them by the gods they pledge to serve. Warlocks gain their magic from higher beings—other than deities—that may not be of the same plane (i.e., demons and similar creatures). Druids attune themselves to the natural world and wield the power of nature. And bards wield magic through art (traditionally music, but Tamora Pierce's Circle of Magic series portrays mages wielding magic through dance, weaving, metalcraft, and other arts).

DEFINING LAWS FOR THE READER

How you set up a world at the beginning of a story creates a contract between you and the reader, providing a foundation for the rest of the story. If you break the natural laws later on, it can disrupt a reader's immersion in the story and break their trust.

Most of the time, I do not recommend spelling out the natural laws of your world for the reader. In most cases, they are implied through the actions of the characters. Sometimes, a student character—someone who is learning about how a certain part of the world works—can provide a vehicle for dispensing information. However the reader learns about the way the world works, it is important to note that a little information goes a long way and that layering information slowly over time helps pique the reader's curiosity without overloading them.

What part does nature play in your story?
Is it shown through weather, plants, or
moon cycles? Is each occurrence of
nature helpful or dangerous?

TIDBIT 2

NATURE

**What part does nature play in your story?
Is it shown through weather, plants, or
moon cycles? Is each occurrence of
nature helpful or dangerous?**

Nature is pervasive, both in the real world and in stories. Even when we try to cover it up or replace it with concrete, metal, or other technology, it often finds ways to prevail or "retaliate," like weeds popping up through sidewalks or massive storms threatening large populations and infrastructure. In stories, nature can play an important part, whether positive or negative, or simply provide a setting in which the story takes place.

NATURE AS SETTING

The setting of most stories begins with nature. What types of terrain and climate characterize the story setting? If there is infrastructure, does it work alongside the existing nature, or is nature altered to fit the infrastructure? How does technology or magic affect the natural world? Is there something about the terrain that requires a specific means of travel, such as boats to travel across water or starships to travel through space?

While a story may only hint at its setting, nature can also be important in shaping a culture. Nomads traveling through a desert may clothe themselves from head to toe to protect themselves from sun, sand, and more. Life by a sea or other large body of water can lead to forms of travel created to suit the water, while life in a forest may lead to homes and roads built within the canopy.

Nature can also heavily influence a story. The length of a journey may be determined as much by the variety of terrain to be traversed as by the distance. A threat posed by a specific form of nature (plants, natural disasters, etc.) or even a threat to nature itself (society-induced climate change or plant life endangered by social lifestyles) may instigate a quest for solutions that is central to the plot.

NATURE IN HIGH-TECHNOLOGY STORIES

Even in science fiction with all-consuming technology, nature should be present in some form. In a city of metal without any kind of greenery, the lives of the people within it would still be affected by climate, weather, and astronomical phenomena. Additionally, in the absence of greenery, the general process of breathing would have to be dealt with, as well as sources for food and water.

Similar concerns would plague life on a starship. However, characters on a starship would also need to deal with the harsh environment of space and perhaps unknown natural phenomena of unfamiliar planets. Time and again, shows like *Star Trek* have explored planets other than Earth from the human perspective, and oftentimes the presented threat stems from a planet's nature, rather than technology or another culture.

BACKGROUND VERSUS STORY ELEMENT

There are times when nature may not play a significant role in a story. For example, nature may only be seen in the void through which a spaceship travels or implied through the survival of characters who need food, water, and air to live. There is nothing wrong with leaving nature as a background force, but showing glimpses of it throughout a story can add depth to the story and world.

Nature can also make a powerful story element. Perhaps there is a wide, rushing river or seemingly impossible mountain range that stands in the path of the characters and needs to be traversed or circumvented. Maybe a storm or some harsh climate threatens the livelihood of the characters. Perhaps a strange plant has been introduced to the environment and proves a threat to the local vegetation, livestock, or people.

Nature can play various parts, with varying importance, within a story. These roles can run from the implied source of necessary supplies or glimpses of a natural structure characters can interact with, to influential pieces of minor subplots or the source of a story's main conflict.

HELPING HAND VERSUS OBSTACLE TO OVERCOME

Whatever form nature takes in a story, there is always a possibility that it is more than a neutral piece of the setting. While nature itself rarely holds love or hate for the societies that live within it, its very presence (or absence, in cases of nature that is waning or has been wiped out) can provide an advantage or hindrance to the characters of a story. Let us look, for example, at nature as shown through a storm, a plant, and the phases of the moon.

A storm is generally considered a natural weather phenomenon, but even an ordinary storm can increase tension or provide a helping hand. For a group traveling on foot, a storm can provide a threat of treacherous roads, illness caused by damp and cold, or simply a delay that could make the difference between success and failure. On the other hand, a storm may also provide a diversion for someone running for their life or a way to travel unseen for those whose business is covert and secret.

When it comes to plants, a single plant or type of plant may seem uninteresting. But when that plant is one of a kind or appears in a place where it does not belong or that is otherwise barren, that plant can become highly important. A new plant can become invasive, choking out the naturally local vegetation or acting as a poison for livestock or people. A one-of-a-kind plant can end up being a necessary cure, and an unusual plant can offer a new source of income. Then there are stories like "Jack and the Beanstalk," in which the plant can be both beneficial and dangerous.

While the phases of the moon may seem innocuous, there are many things tied to moon phases that can affect a story. The most common, and possibly a dangerous one, is the idea of werewolves shifting from human to their more animalistic forms on the full moon. However, the moon drives the tides and possibly people's moods, and both magic and technology can be tied to moon cycles, depending on the world.

The presence of nonhumans in your story's world, such as plants, animals, or artificial intelligence, can enhance the setting's realism. What nonhumans do you integrate into your story?

TIDBIT 3

NONHUMANS

The presence of nonhumans in your story's world, such as plants, animals, or artificial intelligence, can enhance the setting's realism. What nonhumans do you integrate into your story?

The presence of nonhumans (or nonsentients, in stories with nonhuman races) enriches the background and structure of the world where your characters reside. Plants, animals, and other nonsentients can add depth and dimension that bring your world to life, drawing your reader even deeper into the story.

PLANTS AND FUNGI

Plants and fungi are persistent forms of life and can be found in most places where life is present, even under the sea and among the steel and concrete of big cities. The role they play in stories can be just as varied. Perhaps they are a lone comfort in a place almost entirely void of nature. Maybe they offer shade or a place to hide. They might provide food or a form of travel. Their purpose in the story could also be greater, such as the source of a needed medicine or a barrier that threatens characters' survival or goals.

ANIMALS

Animals, whether they appear as wild or domesticated, are nearly as existent and persistent as plants and fungi, and sometimes, characters in a story are more likely to interact with animals than plants. Whether they appear as sources of food, pests (e.g., insects or rodents), pets, beasts of burden, or threats, animals can help shape the world your characters move through. Animals may also be a good source for materials, such as wool, hides, or bones. Consider how animals might appear in your story to better represent your world.

GOLEMS, ROBOTS, AND ARTIFICIAL INTELLIGENCE

Natural life is not the only "life" to be considered when creating a world. Manmade life—objects given the form of life (human or animal, perhaps) and that move, seem intelligent, or seem to have their own personalities—may exist for stories based in modern Earth or magically/technologically advanced worlds. Since the mid-twentieth century, robots of varying quality have been created to entertain us or ease our way of life. Over the ensuing decades, the definition of artificial intelligence has changed as widely available technologies accomplish an increasing range of higher-level tasks.

If your story bleeds into more advanced science fiction, perhaps these ideas can be taken to the next level by filling the lives of the characters with various forms of artificial life or advancing the capabilities of such technologies. If your story is heavy in magic, magically created creatures, such as golems, can fill a similar role to aid your characters.

MICROORGANISMS

Then there are the life-forms your characters may never see but can definitely be affected by. Microorganisms, such as bacteria, viruses, pollen, spores, and tiny seeds, can play minor and major roles in stories. By knowing how such things are transmitted or dispersed, what effects they might have on different individuals, and how much time passes between when they settle and when their impact is felt, you can determine the types of roles they might play in your story and how to depict the outcomes.

MONSTERS, ALIENS, AND MYTHICAL CREATURES

Other nonhumans that might appear in stories include monsters, aliens, and mythical creatures. In stories based on Earth, in which such creatures may or may not exist, mythology and legends surrounding these creatures can add depth to the world you're creating. Even hints of related activity (e.g., spirit boards, spirit mediums, ghost hunting) can add shades and tones to your world and pull your readers further in.

BLEEDING INTO SENTIENCE

The lines between sentience (intelligent life) and non-sentience for nonhumans can become very blurred, especially in stories that fall into the realm of speculative fiction. Many works exist that feature sentient versions of each type of nonhuman listed here. My own Evon series features two horses and a tree who are sentient because of the magic that fills or surrounds them. Robots and artificial intelligence have been featured as sentient beings (and distinct life-forms) throughout the history of science fiction. And characters who fall into the category of monster, alien, or mythical creature are quite often portrayed as sentient.

If you feature nonhumans as sentient creatures, consider looking at them as a separate culture. As you read through the rest of these tidbits, apply them to the society of your sentient nonhumans as much as the main society of your world.

NONSENTIENT LIFE IN STORIES

Whatever nonhumans you decide to portray, sentient

characters should not be the only forms of life in your story—unless, of course, they literally are the only life in the world of your story (e.g., a single person in a contained, self-sustaining spaceship—but even that kind of environment might contain an advanced computer and microorganisms). Help your reader better visualize and understand your world by showing them how your sentient characters interact with other life-forms. Show how emotional connections may or may not be made between sentient characters and the nonsentients around them. Show how your sentient characters might depend on the nonsentients—physically, mentally, and emotionally—regardless of whether they realize or acknowledge that dependence.

PART II

POLITICAL ASPECTS

What form does politics take in your story?
Does it show up on a small scale or large?
Who represents it: monarchs, judges, police?
Does anyone stand against it?

Tidbit 4

Politics

What form does politics take in your story?
Does it show up on a small scale or large?
Who represents it: monarchs, judges, police?
Does anyone stand against it?

Politics appears more often in stories than some people may think. Usually, when I ask writers how politics is portrayed in their worlds and stories, many think only of the larger government of the country or world where their story takes place or in reference to the politics of current events. But like so many things in writing, that is only the tip of the political iceberg.

Defining Politics

While politics can be defined as related to government, there is a larger sense of the word that deals with the general relations between people within a society. This greater sense of politics can be seen in the interconnection of politics and many social issues.

Politics goes beyond the president, monarch, emperor, or other leader of the larger community. Politics includes judges, lawyers, police, secret police, and federal and state agencies. It encompasses events, like riots, rebellions, and protests, as well as the laws (written or otherwise) that guide a country's citizens and how those laws are enforced.

Outside of government, the word is often used mainly in situations revolving around power, especially in comparison to others. Politics comprises the hierarchical structure of an organization and how different members interact. For example, "office politics" is a common term used in modern business environments to refer to bids for power within a company's hierarchy.

POLITICS AS GOVERNMENT

Whether or not governmental politics appears directly in a story, the type of government, both at a country and local level, can influence the story's shape. What form does the government take? Does it have a single ruler, or is it more democratic, with representatives for smaller groups? How strict is the government, and how involved is it in the lives of individuals? Do characters feel its effect through taxation, inspections, or seizures? For example, do government officials conduct raids for activities they deem suspicious or threatening?

Alternatively, the government may be very hands-off, leaving citizens to fend for themselves. If so, how does this lack of government interference affect citizens? Are there one or more groups, such as gangs, militia, or crime syndicates, that have stepped into the power vacuum provided by such a government policy?

Another aspect of government to consider is how it is influenced by religion or economics. Perhaps the government is strictly governed by the laws of a specific religion, pushing nonbelievers or worshippers of other faiths to hide or flee. The government may also be heavily driven by the economy, with corporations or profits steering laws and the actions of politicians more than anything else.

POLITICS AS SOCIAL STRUCTURE

Politics can go hand in hand with the social aspects of a world or story, especially with regards to institutions like slavery, caste systems, or other hierarchical social systems reinforced by governmental law and enforced by governmental bodies (judges, police, etc.). Sometimes, though, it may be the reversal of such systems—when laws name and define what was previously assumed or ignored in order to enact change—that brings the social aspect blatantly into the political arena.

The social aspects of politics often appear within stories without being considered political. How one group of people is treated by another, whether based on race, religion, gender / gender identity, sexual preferences, or birth within a particular family, may be seen as religious or social. However, if power is involved, especially the power of one group over another, then it can be defined as politics as well.

POLITICS IN OTHER ARENAS

Politics can be found in organizations as well as the government of a country. Whether you look at a religious organization, a company, a community, or even a large family, each group has a purpose and the means of carrying it out (written or otherwise). Each also has a structure that defines how individuals interact and how the organization may react to outside threats, relationships, and other influences.

While larger governments can define the general environment of a character's life, it is the smaller arenas where such a character is most likely to become directly involved in politics. Such politics might appear in the way a character deals with people who hold power over them (e.g., a boss, gang leader, or family matriarch or patriarch) or with people over whom they hold power (e.g., employees, informants, or younger family members).

POLITICS THROUGH CORRUPTION

As ideal as it may be to write about politics free from corruption, politics usually relates to power, and as John Dalberg-Acton is credited with saying, "power tends to corrupt and absolute power corrupts absolutely."

While some people are capable of holding onto

their moral compass as their power grows, that is not always the case. Some believe the addition of power reveals a person's true nature, that the growth of their power frees them from bending to the will of those who previously held power over them.

What would this corruption look like in a story? It could take many forms: bribes paid to government officials or guards, judges preferring one side of a case over the other based on their personal beliefs rather than actual law, or guards beating prisoners or otherwise lording power over them, whether verbally, physically, or sexually.

In stories, widespread corruption can also provide a setting for a bright star of hope. Some people can hold true to their morality, even in positions of power. The lone good cop, honest politician, or generous noble can make a compelling main or supporting character. The character arc of losing one's way and then finding it again can also be powerful where politics and corruption are concerned.

When different cultures interact, they can either clash or cooperate. How do the cultures in your story generally interact? Are there any incidents in the story that are exceptions to the general rule?

TIDBIT 5

MULTICULTURAL INTERACTION

When different cultures interact, they can either clash or cooperate. How do the cultures in your story generally interact? Are there any incidents in the story that are exceptions to the general rule?

Oftentimes, stories include different cultures, which may be represented by separate countries, separate religions, or separate races. When multiple cultures exist and meet, how they interact can vary widely depending on the cultures involved and their views of people who are different.

TRADE

The simplest form of interaction between different

cultures is trade. Most societies are not self-sufficient, especially when viewed at local levels. Even an autonomous culture may find that another culture possesses additional resources that can increase the quality of its citizens' lives. Whether a society needs water, increased variety of food, art, building materials, or other resources, building a trade relationship with another culture can help the society procure these.

Trade, however, does not need to be limited to physical goods. Information can easily be exchanged in these kinds of relationships. Such information may concern the lay of the land, weather patterns, survival techniques, forms of technology or magic, or political climates. Remember, too, that what one culture holds in high regard, another may view as mundane.

CONQUEST, SUBJUGATION, AND COLONIZATION

Sometimes, trade agreements are not enough to satisfy a society. The desire for more land and resources or the desire to spread its culture or beliefs may push a society to conquer other cultures. This can happen when one society discovers a culture that is less tech-nologically or magically advanced.

While conquest can lead to combat, war is not the only way for a society to subjugate another culture. Especially when the need to control ties to a desire to spread a set of beliefs, a society may find it easier to approach the other culture as a well-meaning teacher, sharing goods and knowledge even as they take over.

WAR

As mentioned before, the desire to conquer can lead to war. However, hostilities can stem from other interactions between cultures as well. Two cultures might battle over uninhabited land or unclaimed resources. Conflict might begin over differing reli-gious, economic, or sociopolitical views. One culture might even go to war against a conquering society in order to protect those being subjugated. War can also stem from other circumstances, including a desire for revenge, injured pride, a desire for justice or equality, or a desire for independence.

ALLIANCE

On the opposite end of the spectrum from war is alliance. While alliances can be formed between cultures to aid each other during conflicts with another culture, alliances are not restricted to such circumstances. Two or more cultures can enter into an alliance for any mutually beneficial endeavor, which is often a sign the cultures view each other as potential equals. Cultures within an alliance might help each other in times of need, hold long-term trade agreements, share knowledge, and work together to further various projects.

COMPETITION

Speaking of projects, two cultures might find themselves in competition with each other, friendly or otherwise. This might stem from trying to be the first to reach a certain level of technology or magic or to solve a certain problem. An example of this is the space race between the United States and the Soviet Union that lasted from the 1950s into the 1970s.

COHABITATION, SYMBIOSIS, AND INTEGRATION

Multiple cultures may settle in the same place, live together side by side, and integrate their different beliefs and customs. Ideally, this would be mutually beneficial for all cultures involved (consider the relationship between the sea anemone and the clownfish). However, the differences between the cultures might lead to socioeconomic inequality and perhaps slavery or war.

If the world you are creating has a diverse population within one area, consider the history of how it came to be that way. Was the area colonized by outsiders? Perhaps other peoples were brought as slaves or a paid labor force. Was there mutual agreement between different cultures as the area was settled?

EXCEPTIONS TO THE RULES

Stories are driven by tension, which is frequently created by exceptions to the rules rather than the status quo. Once you have settled how different cultures relate to each other, consider the pockets within those societies that do not conform to the general rules. If two cultures are at war, can friendship or love be found between individuals from each? If two cultures are allied, what might happen if a single event threatens the alliance?

Look to outliers of your cultures for the big stories of your world. Change begets stories, and even the smallest change in the relationships between cultures can prove to be a powerful tale.

PART III

ECONOMIC ASPECTS

How does economy play into your story?
What kind of tender does your society
use? Do people barely scrape by, or is
money always available? Why?

TIDBIT 6

ECONOMY

How does economy play into your story? What kind of tender does your society use? Do people barely scrape by, or is money always available? Why?

However inconvenient it may be for us as writers, our characters need to be able to provide for their own basic needs: food, clothing, lodgings, and everything beyond. Whether they come from old money, live off the land, work a job of some kind, or struggle to make ends meet, your characters live in some form of economy and must have a way to navigate it, even if they do not do it well.

TYPES OF TENDER

One of the most visible forms economy may take in a story is the type of tender characters use and how they use it. If the story is based in a real-world setting, this decision is easy; all you need to know is where and when the story takes place and then select the appropriate exchange medium: US dollars, British pounds, Japanese yen, Chinese yuan, etc.

Most modern-day economies use replacement currency: paper and coin money that represent a government-backed value versus the actual worth of the currency's fabrication material. Some economies might base the representative value of their money on another form of wealth, like the gold and silver standard once used by the United States. A currency's value might also be measured against the value of other replacement currency, similar to the ever-fluc-tuating exchange rates of today's markets.

But paper and coin money are not the only possible tender to consider for a story, especially when dealing with speculative fiction. For those characters who live off the land, a barter or trade system might be more applicable than the use of any tender. For stories taking place in a larger setting that may not support simple bartering, the use of gems or precious metals with a set worth could be more applicable. Coins made of gold, silver, or copper would have set values determined by their material and weight. The phrase "worth its weight in gold" speaks to this kind of tender.

Science fiction opens up the possibility for another kind of tender: electronic. Several sci-fi stories use "credits" as a wide-ranging, generic currency that is easy to use without too much explanation. No physical currency or commodities are exchanged because the values are recorded and stored in microchips or other electronic devices.

Even with all these possibilities, there is something to be said for having a unique monetary tender. Sometimes a specific commodity becomes so important to an economy that it becomes the currency. One such commodity that has acted as a tender throughout human history is salt, which has a history of importance going back several thousand years.

But salt is just one example of an important commodity becoming the tender for an economy. In fact, such commodities don't need to be restricted to the physical. One of my favorite unique tenders comes from the movie *In Time*, in which time has become the currency of the world. In this movie, genetic engineering has made it possible for people to stop aging and live forever—assuming they can obtain the time to do so, whether through work, investment, gambling, stealing, or being born into a wealthy family.

ECONOMIC CYCLE: WORK AND EXPENSES

As long as characters are living creatures, they will always have expenses of some kind that need to be taken care of. Even characters who are not quite living, such as machines or the undead, would still need repairs or the satiation of certain appetites. And anyone living within some form of society needs to be able to afford to live within it (or appear to, at least) to get along without struggle.

When contemplating the daily lives of your characters, you want to consider not only the basics (lodgings, clothing, and food) but also the luxuries (special clothing, jewelry, entertainment, or art). How extravagantly do they live? And how does that compare with the work they perform to make money? Is there a discrepancy between their earnings and expenses, and how does that show in the story?

Other expenses your characters may encounter that indirectly relate to their basic needs or luxuries are fees imposed by governments or other organizations. Sales tax on purchases, income tax on money earned, tariffs and duties on imported/exported goods—all of these are costs to consider. Such things may seem trivial, but for a character who deals in trade, for example, tariffs and duties may take more of their profit than they can afford to lose.

ECONOMIC STRUGGLE AND DISHONESTY

Sometimes the tension or conflict within a story comes from a character's struggle to survive within the economy of their world. Perhaps they struggle to find a legal job that can support their basic needs. Maybe they've lost their home and struggle from day to day to survive, taking what they can get, legally or otherwise. And sometimes, a character's interests and capabilities lead them to a life that is more dishonest than others.

Whatever the reason, dishonesty in economy can

appear in different ways in stories. From con men who cheat to outright thieves who steal, characters can use both their brains and their brawn to obtain money that does not rightfully belong to them.

In reference to legal tender, characters can steal physical currency or perform sleight of hand to make it seem like they paid more than they did. When dealing with gold coins, merchants can bite into a coin to make sure of its purity (as gold is a soft metal, the bite would leave a mark), hoping to prevent themselves from being conned into accepting fake coins. Similarly, a merchant might weigh the coins to make sure pieces have not been shaved off, which would lessen the coins' value.

Part IV

Religious Aspects

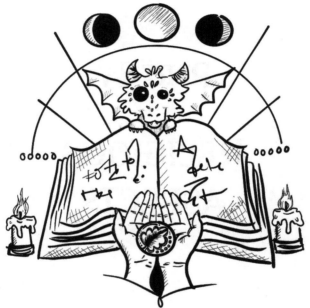

How does religion appear in your story? Are
your characters blatantly or subtly religious?
Are they atheistic or simply indifferent?

TIDBIT 7

RELIGION

**How does religion appear in your story? Are
your characters blatantly or subtly religious?
Are they atheistic or simply indifferent?**

Part of human nature, it seems, is to believe in
something larger than oneself, whatever form that
may take. Sometimes that belief is blatant, shown in
the clothes and ornaments worn or the gestures and
rituals performed. At other times, it is seen only in
how a person interacts with others or what holds the
most importance in that person's life.

In the same way, the characters in a story have
their own beliefs and show them in their own ways.
And just as they do in real life, people of the same religious belief often show their belief in different ways.

DRAWING RELIGION FROM THE SPIRITUAL

As the writer of your story, you define the spiritual reality of your world. Depending on the way your world works, though, the mortals most likely have no way of knowing the spiritual truth. That is where religion comes in.

Whether created by a group of average people, by a single ruler claiming to be a god, or by people who have true spiritual gifts, religions are the mortal interpretation of the spiritual reality. For stories based in the real world, religions may be predefined. Like economy, you only need to consider the where and when to identify all the possible religions.

Speculative fiction opens the door to an even greater range of possibilities. Fantasy and science fiction allow you to create new religions, either cobbled together from existing ideas or formed from seemingly new ones. Science fiction based on a futuristic Earth can weave an evolution of religions from what we currently know to what might occur.

Even in stories that contain characters who possess spiritual gifts or are actual deities, the religions may not match the spiritual reality. Religion is the mortal interpretation, so those with spiritual gifts may not be able to correctly interpret what they see or hear. Meanwhile, deities may not tell the full truth—because of pride, a desire for power, a lack of understanding on the mortals' part, or something else.

TYPES OF RELIGION

Many types of religion exist throughout the world, offering a plethora of possibilities for stories. While I recommend researching existing religions to help portray what you want in your story, we can cover the basics here.

Generally, religions fall under monotheism, polytheism, agnosticism, and atheism. Monotheism centers on a single deity. Polytheism usually includes a pantheon of deities of varying degrees of importance and power. Agnosticism is the belief that whatever divine power may exist is unknowable and undefinable. And atheism is the belief that deities simply do not exist.

These general ideas can be adapted and intermingled. Perhaps only one deity is worshipped regularly, while lesser deities or spirits are called on for specific activities. Maybe a higher power is not acknowledged, but a widespread ability to see or hear spirits allows for the acceptance of souls.

Also, what one religion believes about itself may differ from how it is perceived by outsiders or people of other religions. For example, while all Abrahamic religions (Judaism, Christianity, and Islam) may be considered monotheism by their followers, there are some who consider Christianity a type of polytheism due to the three-part nature of the Christian God (the Father, the Son, and the Holy Spirit).

Types of Religion

Monotheism—belief that there is only one god.

Polytheism—belief that there are multiple gods of varying power and importance. Each god usually has their own domain.

Agnosticism—belief that the existence of a higher power cannot be known by human intelligence.

Atheism—belief that gods do not exist.

DEPTH OF RELIGION

Once you have defined the religion of your world, the next step is deciding how deeply ingrained it is within the characters' lives. Just as every person in the real world has different experiences with religion, so will each of your characters.

We can start with the basics to determine where your characters stand when it comes to religion. Is religion practiced openly or in secret? Is religious practice mandated by the government, or are people allowed to do as they wish? How strict is the religion with regards to exploring beliefs and other religions? Are people allowed to be indifferent to the religion, or are they forced to practice it or face exile?

By integrating the answers to these questions with the personalities and life experiences of your characters, you can better understand where they stand with religion. Were they fully accepted by their religion growing up, leading them to form a strong faith? Did they grow up with criticism and hate, leading them to either seek acceptance through other religions or simply rebel? Or perhaps they are simply not interested in religion one way or the other but still carry certain mannerisms that were instilled within them growing up.

SIGNS OF RELIGION

Every religion bears its own mixture of rituals, ceremonies, sayings, images, symbols, artifacts, and more. Each has its own rules related to morality, people's actions, and how to venerate its deities. Depending on the depth of religion in your characters' lives, one or more of these features may appear in the story, either to add depth to the world or to add a twist to the story.

Examples of such signs of religion are endless. A Christian—or even former Christian—may make the sign of the cross before a meal as thanks. Perhaps a character carries a symbol of their faith, such as a cross, Star of David, or ankh. Characters might also pray at certain times of the day or attend a religious service every week.

PART V

SOCIAL ASPECTS

What does the social hierarchy look like in your story? Is there just one, or are there multiple hierarchies? Where do your characters fall within them?

TIDBIT 8

SOCIAL HIERARCHY

What does the social hierarchy look like in your story? Is there just one, or are there multiple hierarchies? Where do your characters fall within them?

Most societies have some form of social hierarchy, regardless of whether it is consciously defined. This structure provides a cultural or societal framework that characterizes people and determines with whom they interact, how they interact, and which occupations or material goods and services they can access. Even if the structure is not defined in your story, it can greatly affect the actions of the characters within it.

Defining a Hierarchy

Though social hierarchies generally determine how people are treated socially, hierarchies can be defined by the social, economic, political, or intellectual aspects of the world. Where a person falls in this hierarchy may be determined by race, gender, age, economic status, intelligence, or some other form of power the culture deems important, such as magical power or the technological makeup of their body.

Social hierarchies often date back to the beginning of a culture or country. Because of this, the reasons behind the hierarchy may not be immediately apparent when looking at it within a story's time frame. After centuries or millennia, the underlying divisions have most likely become systemic, and the tiers may appear to be related to something else.

For example, consider a social hierarchy in which the rich hold the most power and those with little power struggle daily to stay alive. While such a structure may appear to be based solely on economics, analyzing the demographics of the different tiers could indicate otherwise. Perhaps those with the most money are also those of a particular race, gender, religion, or magic/science level. It is also possible that people of one race, gender, religion, or magic/science level can move between different social tiers more easily than others. Looking for individuals who stand out as exceptions to the norm can help you define these rules.

If a story takes place closer to the creation of a social hierarchy, the hierarchy may be unstable. In such a case, the hierarchy previously in place should be considered, as those who rebel against a new social hierarchy may advocate for the return of the old.

MOVEMENT BETWEEN TIERS

Are people able to move from one social tier to another in the social hierarchy of your story? Depending on how the hierarchy is defined, this could range from easy to impossible.

Most characters are born into a specific social tier of a hierarchy. Generally, this would be determined by who their parents are; however, if tiers are defined by intelligence, age, or job, this may not be true. Such an exception could lead to the possibility that children are not raised by their birth family, which would add another dynamic to the story.

For hierarchies based on economic status or political power, movement may be fairly easy, assuming all other aspects are equal and prejudice does not prevent people of certain races, genders, religions, or magic/science levels from changing their economic or political status without undue burden. Even when such prejudices are present, there may be people who move between tiers despite the social restrictions, depending on the strictness of the hierarchy. Such people may have the power to make changes, or they may simply be viewed by those of their new level as interlopers.

For stricter hierarchies based on race, gender, or other seemingly unchangeable factors, movement between tiers may still be possible. Marriage, change of career, and education are some possibilities. Then there are characters who resort to deceit. Pretending to be of another gender, race, or religion can be a powerful setup for story and character arcs.

Pros and Cons of Different Tiers

A quick glance at most social hierarchies may indicate

that the highest tier is always the best, with access to the greatest luxuries and most freedoms. While those in the lowest tier most likely have the hardest time surviving without pain and fear of starvation or death, higher tiers may have a different kind of disadvantage.

Certain expectations generally come with the higher tiers of a social hierarchy, such as how a person acts, who they marry, how they speak, where they go, or what they do with their lives. These expectations can be interpreted as restrictive, particularly by idealists who are knowledgeable about greater freedoms and those who have moved up the hierarchy and were unfamiliar with the subsequent expectations.

Restrictive expectations can be especially pertinent for subsets within higher tiers. For example, a common idea among noble families within some social hierarchies is that men are allowed more freedoms than women. In such cases, the men may gripe about their responsibilities, while the women may chafe and wish for more opportunities, whether in travel, business, or love and marriage.

CHARACTERS WITHIN SOCIAL HIERARCHIES

Once you define the social hierarchies for your world, you then need to decide where each of your characters fall within them. How do their social positions affect their interaction with each other? Do any of your characters rebel against the hierarchy, and why? Have any of them found their way into a tier they were not born into, and if so, how?

It is always good to include characters from different social tiers throughout a story. Good representation adds depth to your world and opens possibilities for new tension and conflict as the beliefs, limitations, and expectations of one tier clash with those of another. While social hierarchy does not have to fuel the main conflict of the story, even minor tension among friends based on differing lifestyles can drive a story forward and hold your reader's interest.

How do characters in your story view strangers?
Do they embrace them, are they wary of them,
or do they downright hate them?

TIDBIT 9

STRANGERS

**How do characters in your story view strangers?
Do they embrace them, are they wary of them,
or do they downright hate them?**

Strangers can be classified in two ways when it comes to how your characters treat them. By one definition, strangers are just people your characters have never met before. Such strangers can easily become acquaintances with only a little interaction. The second classification refers to people who are different from your characters. Depending on your characters' history or culture, how they view these two types of strangers may coincide or be miles apart.

COME AND BE WELCOME

As a society, the people you write about may accept strangers with open arms, both those they do not know and those who are different from them. Such acceptance may include taking what they say at face value without looking for lies or providing them with food, drink, and other supplies if they are in need. It can also include providing a ride or a place to board for the night or simply giving directions.

Such acceptance may stem from a general belief in the good of humanity (or sentience or life, depending on the beings your stories feature). Such acceptance can also spring from a trust in higher beings, such as deities, or a higher power, such as fate, that protects them from any harm as long as they continue to live their lives well. It might also be based on a belief that doing good for others will encourage similar behavior in return.

Another possible explanation for accepting those who are unfamiliar stems from mythical or magical reasoning. Some cultures believe that beings such as gods or the fae will disguise themselves as mortals in need to test a person's hospitality. In these cultures, to scorn such a stranger is to risk their wrath, which could come in the form of barren land or livestock, plague, or even death. To accept a stranger and treat them kindly may invite a blessing upon the land and the family of the one who treated them well.

Do Not Talk to Strangers

On the other hand, many societies are not so accepting of strangers, or at least, not without wariness. This distrust can show in many ways: ignoring a stranger's request for help or supplies, turning the stranger away and denying them services, or providing help based on a condition or only out of politeness.

Societies that view strangers in this way may believe that good intentions must be proven, that unknown humans (or other life) are inherently dangerous and evil, or simply that the world itself is perilous. Safety can be a consideration, but the desire for security may not be the only influence.

This particular view of strangers often illustrates the distinction between strangers who are unknown and strangers who are conspicuously different. Even in societies where people are wary of those they do not know, common ground can ease that wariness. If a person finds they have something in common with a stranger (e.g., skin color, speech patterns, religion, politics, economic level), then they are more likely to believe they share other commonalities.

Alternatively, if a person focuses on a specific difference that makes the stranger stand out, then even a shared experience may not be enough to quell their wariness. While stereotypes may not be ideal to live or write by, they can be important in understanding the actions and reactions of a character who believes in them or has such stereotypes ingrained in their mindset.

KILL OR BE KILLED

There are some worlds and societies where encountering strangers with wariness is not considered enough. In these, a stranger might be attacked or killed on sight. In the case of those who doubt they can overpower the stranger, the reaction might, instead, be to hide or flee.

In such worlds or societies, an unknown person—whether or not they are different—may be considered dangerous and a threat. Postapocalyptic tales often use this concept, playing on the premise that a lack of law leads to violence and other amoral activity.

This reaction to strangers could also be based on a general isolationist lifestyle, in which only the familiar is considered safe. War and plague can lead to this behavior, as well as the belief that others are inferior and, therefore, dangerous.

CANNOT SEE THE FOREST FOR THE TREES

However a society in general views strangers, a single individual within that society may have divergent beliefs. These opinions could be based on the individual's history (e.g., trauma resulting from a dangerous encounter or good memories of a helpful stranger) or their personality (e.g., optimism versus pessimism, naïveté versus cynicism).

Regarding a society's view of strangers, another idea to consider is the possibility of a temporary shift in societal beliefs. Even a society that is open to strangers can become wary in the face of a murder or other violent act. Anyone new to an area or otherwise unknown might be the first suspected, rather than those who are familiar.

TWO SIDES OF THE SAME COIN

No matter how strangers are viewed by the societies and characters you write, keep in mind that all parties involved in an interaction carry their own assumptions about strangers. These beliefs would influence people in need as much as those they might approach. Would they trust a stranger to provide help or try to solve the problem on their own? When two people meet for the first time, consider how each will react to the other and how the environment affects the situation. Those open to strangers might be uncomfortable in an unfamiliar setting, while someone who is wary of strangers may feel more in control in their own territory.

What does family mean in your story? Do
people stay with blood relatives, are they
forced into other kinds of familial units, or
do they define their own family?

TIDBIT 10

FAMILY

What does family mean in your story? Do people stay with blood relatives, are they forced into other kinds of familial units, or do they define their own family?

Barring unique circumstances, most characters have a family of origin, a family that raises them, and at least one family they choose. Sometimes, they are all the same; sometimes, they are all different. Regardless, family usually has some importance to a character—good or bad—that influences the way they think and act.

ℐMPORTANCE OF ℱAMILY

Family means different things to different people, even within the same family unit. Family's importance to a character generally comes from how they were raised, the individual relationships they have with specific family members, and the values they hold compared to the values their family holds.

Those characters who hold family in high regard or connect closely with certain family members may be influenced by these sentiments. Perhaps they seek to honor their family through actions that bring the entire family power, money, or respect. They may even be driven to stand between their family and a threat, protecting them against all odds or taking a stance against someone more powerful, such as an authority to which they hold a lesser or conflicting loyalty.

But family can also be a burden, or even a threat, to a character. Those raised in abusive families or quelled by their families growing up may flee from the idea of family at the earliest possibility. Their ability to trust others or themselves can be degraded, leaving them to believe that being alone is better than the risk of being hurt or subjugated again. On the other hand, characters may seek out those who will accept them for who they are and form a new family with those they have come to trust, possibly without consciously trying to.

Family's importance to a character does not have to remain stagnant throughout a story. As a character grows and changes, so too can their view of family. Conceivably, they could start by fleeing from the only family they have known, seeking to be alone. But through their experiences, they might end up gathering close those they have come to trust and love.

BLOOD FAMILY

Any creature of biological origin is going to have a blood family, a family of origin. Whether a character ever knows their blood family depends on the story and the world in which it is set.

For those who know their blood family and are raised by them, another question to consider is the size of the family. Are they raised exclusively by their nuclear family (i.e., their parents and siblings)? Or are they raised by, or within, a large, extended family, including grandparents, aunts, uncles, and cousins?

How many siblings do they have? Are they particularly close to any family members? Are there family members they do not get along with?

Some of these questions tie back to the nature of the world. Do the families of your world stay together for as long as possible, forming large, sprawling family units in which it is rare to lose track of a child, even when they are grown? Or does your world support individuals leaving their homes as early as possible, setting off on their own to forge their own lives? Does your world enable families to have large numbers of children? Or do they struggle to have even one or two?

SOCIALLY FORMED FAMILY

Sometimes, a story and the world it is set in do not support a character being raised by their blood family. Parents may die when the character is young. Or perhaps the character is born into a world that does not allow children to be raised by their blood family.

For a character who loses their parents at a young age, there are several possibilities. They might be raised in an orphanage or a foster home or be adopted by another family. Alternatively, they could end up on the streets and be raised by gangs or others like themselves.

It may not be just a single character who is raised by someone other than blood family. There are many stories, especially sci-fi or utopian/dystopian stories, in which society has chosen to produce and raise its children differently. Two that come to mind are *The Giver* and *Brave New World*. In *The Giver*, specific women have the job of bearing children, who are then assigned to nuclear family units to be raised. In *Brave New World*, society creates test-tube babies, who are then raised in nurseries specific to the type of job they are predestined to work.

Another type of family that falls under socially formed, rather than self-defined, is arranged marriages. While arranged marriages can evolve into desired relationships, they are initiated by a character's parents or by society and are not always desired by those within them.

SELF-DEFINED FAMILY

Regardless of who raises a character, the self-defined

family is often the character's most important family. This could be a group of friends who bond over experiences and shared trust, a connection formed through a romantic or close platonic relationship, or a unit created when parents adopt or otherwise take in and care for orphaned children. Self-defined family can even include the family who raises the character, as time and experience confirm its importance to the character and the strength of the relationships within it.

However characters come to define their chosen family, the strong personal relationships forged within them, built on trust and acceptance, are often the ones that characters will fight to protect, no matter the odds that stand against them.

How is Love, platonic or romantic, viewed
in your story? Is it a goal? Is it considered
impossible or taboo? Or is Love a
weakness or obstacle to overcome?

TIDBIT 11

LOVE

How is love, platonic or romantic, viewed in your story? Is it a goal? Is it considered impossible or taboo? Or is love a weakness or obstacle to overcome?

Love is probably the most common theme in stories. Love crops up in almost all genres as main characters and side characters are provided love interests to help keep readers intrigued, tie characters together, and move along both the story and the characters' arcs. What form does love take in your story? How does your world view it, and what are your characters' views and feelings on it, both as an idea and in their life?

Part V: Social Aspects

Romantic versus Platonic

First off, I cannot emphasize enough that romantic love is not the only important love to consider in a story. There is something to be said for the unconditional platonic love between family members (blood or chosen), friends, and people and their pets (friends or family of a different kind, you might say). Platonic love can drive a character to stand by someone when others turn against them—emotionally or violently— or it can push a character to seek out a loved one who has gone missing or secluded themselves for some reason.

That said, there is nothing wrong with incorporating romantic love into a story. All relationships should naturally evolve over the course of a story. If the events of a story and the connection between characters lend themselves to a romantic relationship, then it makes sense to include it. However, do not shoehorn a romantic relationship into a story just for the sake of having one. Romantic relationships for their own sake have become a bit cliché, especially in genres like sci-fi/fantasy adventure.

> ### 8 Types of Love, according to the Greeks

> *Eros*—romantic, passionate love
> *Philia*—affectionate love without attraction
> *Agape*—selfless, universal love
> *Storge*—familial love
> *Mania*—obsessive love
> *Ludus*—playful love
> *Pragma*—enduring love
> *Philautia*—self love, considered the source of
> all other love

STRENGTH VERSUS WEAKNESS

Love can be viewed by individuals and society as either a strength or a weakness. This view can be based on an individual's experiences, consequences encountered by a society, or ideas passed down from one generation to another. These views can also differ at various levels: society as a whole, social groups, familial, and individual.

Oftentimes, the ideas of "love is a weakness" and "the power of love" are pitted against each other. Antagonists often hold the belief that love is a weakness because love is seen as a vulnerability. Not only does love require a character to expose their deepest self to another person, the person they love becomes a potential liability for the character—someone who can be kidnapped, tortured, or simply threatened to force the character to do something.

On the other hand, the power of love has been touted time and again by the "good" sides in stories. The weakness of vulnerability is usually balanced by trust, understanding, and teamwork. Love based on a solid foundation becomes something to rely on, as the support of others with complementary skills strengthens everyone.

Of course, these are not the only types of strength and weakness that may be associated with love. For those who value control, the oft-wild emotions that accompany falling in love can be seen as a weakness or, at the very least, something to be avoided. Cultures that value arranged marriages or connections made for power or money may also view love as an inconvenience, as it can threaten the structure valued by most people.

One-sided love can also be viewed as a weakness, especially when the one who loves spends a lot of their time and energy pining after another. Depending on the situation, this type of love can provide an untimely distraction or a willingness to sacrifice that could cost lives.

Another strength found in love relates more to fantasy genres. Many magics have been attached to love in stories, whether through true love's first kiss or simply the strengthening of power that love provides. If this is something you wish to include in your own story, make sure it fits with the rules you have set for your world.

GOAL VERSUS SIDE EFFECT

You can look at the question of love as goal versus love as side effect from two perspectives: As the writer, do you aim to include love in your story in and of itself, or does love end up being included as a result of the events and connections between the characters? From your characters' points of view, do they actively seek love, or does it evolve naturally as part of the journey they are taking?

Your approach for including love might depend on the genre you are writing. Romance definitely requires that some form of romantic love be included, and some broader genres, like young adult, might frequently involve love, though not necessarily a romantic relationship. For those genres that do not necessitate the inclusion of love, any love that appears should be a natural evolution of events within the story, as characters connect, learn about each other, and grow to trust and care for each other.

For your characters, how they approach love depends more on their individual personalities and backgrounds. If a character comes from a loving family, they may expect to connect with someone and fall in love, to the point that it becomes a priority for them. The reverse could also be true; if a character grows up feeling unloved, they might wish to throw themselves into a relationship to find that desired connection.

Depending on the character's personality, the latter example could also have the opposite result. A lack of love in childhood could lead them to avoid connections and isolate themselves. Such characters can still find their way to love, but it would probably be an experience that sneaks up on them as part of their journey, rather than something they actively seek out or recognize.

What form does marriage and divorce take in
the world of your story? How do characters
celebrate weddings? What about anniversaries?

TIDBIT 12

MARRIAGE

What form does marriage and divorce take in the world of your story? How do characters celebrate weddings? What about anniversaries?

Marriage is the basis for many family units, but it does not take the same form in every culture. Similarly, the beginning of a marriage is not always marked the same way, even within the same culture. And while some might feel it important to mark the strength of a marriage by recognizing each year's anniversary, others might find it trivial or even inapplicable.

FORMS OF MARRIAGE

Marriage is the connection between two or more people, generally for the purpose of forming a family.

Definitions of marriage can fall under legal rulings, religious beliefs, and cultural traditions. Some societies, or parts of a society, might define who can get married—two people of opposite sex or of the same social tier, religion, or race—while others might base marriage on financial stability, ability to have children, or power levels.

The intricacy and length of marriage can also vary. For some, marriage might be a lifelong commitment that restricts the actions of those entering into it (whether sexually, emotionally, financially, politically, or otherwise). Others might be based on a legal contract that defines how the marriage will proceed and, perhaps, end. And in some cases, the connection might simply be an alliance between two families or an agreement to procure offspring, without a permanent union between two or more people.

If your story is based in the real world, I recommend researching the marriages of the area and time period you are writing about to make sure your portrayal of marriage is plausible for the world you have set. For speculative fiction genres, I recommend diving into the different parts of your world—religion, politics, history, sexuality, and other cultural traditions—to come up with a form of marriage that makes sense for the world you have created. This would include the possible reasons for marriage and how the partners interact, as well as any rules regarding the partners' behavior, rights, responsibilities, and freedoms, such as pursuing relationships beyond the marriage, either platonic or sexual.

An example of a sci-fi/fantasy marriage that goes beyond the strict two-person partnership of many human cultures is the Denobulan tradition represented in *Star Trek: Enterprise*. In this series, the ship's doctor, Phlox, often speaks fondly of his three wives, each of whom have three husbands, including him. This intricate marriage structure ensures numerous children and does not restrict the sexual ventures of the individuals within it, should they choose to explore.

CELEBRATING THE BEGINNING

Beginnings are important; this is as true for marriage as for anything else. Weddings are a big part of many cultures throughout the world, so it would most likely be a big part of some cultures within the worlds of your stories.

Regardless of whether marriages are grounded in the legal, religious, or political arenas, many weddings (or their equivalents) consist of large, elaborate celebrations. Oftentimes, weddings incorporate certain ceremonies and rituals with meanings that date back to earlier points of the religion or culture. The original purposes of such traditional aspects might include calling on deities or spirits to bless the union, bringing luck, warding off evil, or promoting unity and fertility. These basics are often dressed up with elaborate clothing, flower arrangements, artwork, food, and more. Such embellishments may be personal to the individuals coming into the union or tie into the practices of each family involved.

On the other hand, a wedding ceremony could be bare and simple, especially in the case of an elopement (in which those intending to wed run away to marry in secret) or a simple legal marriage. In such cases, the only elements required are the basic ceremony and generally a representative (legal, political, or religious) to ensure the marriage is binding.

Even if a wedding never features in the stories you write, knowing how the culture celebrates the beginning of a marriage may help you understand more about the lives of your characters and their culture in general.

MARKING ANNIVERSARIES

In some cultures, marking the anniversaries of a marriage highlights the strength of the union and celebrates the connection between those involved. This celebration might only appear as a small acknowledgment between partners and those close to them. Anniversaries can also be celebrated much more lavishly—with dinners, gifts, or other entertainment. Certain anniversaries can have more significance than others, like those acknowledging twenty-five or fifty years. Depending on the culture, the ruler of a country or locale might join the celebrations.

For less formal marriages, anniversaries might mean very little and, therefore, might not be acknowledged at all.

CLOSE OF A MARRIAGE

Just as the beginnings of marriages vary, so do the ways that marriages close. While the death of a partner can end a union (unless the bond is believed to carry beyond death), a marriage might also be defined for a set amount of time from the outset. A form of divorce or annulment may also be allowed for certain reasons—abuse, adultery, or dishonor.

Some cultures do not allow divorce of any kind. Those that do often have certain requirements that must be fulfilled before the divorce is allowed and then steps that must be taken to finalize the divorce. Most likely, these requirements and steps would be governed by the marriage's original arena: political, legal, religious, economic, or cultural.

What does the culture of childbirth look like in your story? Do the people in your world celebrate birthdays? If so, how? Are any age milestones considered important, or are they all irrelevant?

TIDBIT 13

BIRTH CULTURE

What does the culture of childbirth look like in your story? Do the people in your world celebrate birthdays? If so, how? Are any age milestones considered important, or are they all irrelevant?

The birth of new life is beautiful and complex and is treated differently from one society to another. From a community's treatment of pregnant individuals to the ceremonies that follow a child's birth, the culture of birth can be influenced not only by wider cultural traditions but by religion, politics, economy, and levels of science and magic. Similarly, certain birthdays may be marked as important by a society due to religion, politics, science/magic, or other traditions.

PREGNANCY AND CHILDBIRTH

Bringing a new life into the world can be messy and complicated. Entire books have been written on what to expect during pregnancy, and even with modern science, pregnancy can often lead to difficult consequences, up to and including death for either the parent or child.

For this reason and more, the culture of childbirth cannot be taken lightly in any story. Whether a story celebrates new life, mourns the difficulties in producing it, or does not mention it at all, you should consider the treatment of pregnancy and childbirth within the world of your story with purpose.

For those stories not based in the real world, consider the levels of magic and science within your world and how they might affect the quality of pregnancies and the health of expectant parents and their unborn children. Is there advanced science or magic that could make things easier? How would this compare to those who do not have access to such science or magic?

There is the possibility, too, that the world you are writing in is at a point where pregnancy and childbirth are not completely natural or organic.

Perhaps people are grown from test tubes or created entirely from magic. Such processes can help define the world and society you are writing about. For example, *Brave New World* opens with an entire chapter on the science behind breeding new people.

ENCOURAGING AND PREVENTING PREGNANCY

Intimately tied with the concept of pregnancy are the desire to achieve it and the need to prevent it. Many people want children but have difficulty getting pregnant, while others never want children, for various reasons, yet still want to be intimate with others.

Throughout history, many beliefs have flourished about how to encourage and prevent pregnancy, proven or otherwise. Regardless of whether such beliefs are valid, what matters is that they exist and are practiced in some form by the society you write about. These beliefs can range from prayers to gods, various herbal remedies, and folk techniques to scientific or magical intervention before or after sex.

Also consider how different techniques may be viewed. For example, some religions may ban the use of certain practices for encouraging or preventing pregnancy. The impact of such a ban, including how it may or may not be followed, can be explored.

Even if you do not feature pregnancy or birth in your story, I encourage you to contemplate this topic if you feature sexual relations of any kind. Unwanted pregnancy is a topic common to many cultures. Many stories that feature sex do not normalize contraception of any kind; however, at least mentioning the measures individuals may take to prevent pregnancy—or sexually transmitted diseases—can add to the plausibility of the story.

Expectations Around Pregnancy

How are pregnant individuals expected to act during and after pregnancy in your world? Are they expected to work while pregnant and return to their duties not long after giving birth? Are they expected to rest from a certain point in the pregnancy and for a certain amount of time after giving birth? How do individual characters in your story compare to the expectations of the society they live in?

The question of expectations placed on such

individuals extends beyond just pregnancy and childbirth and into general gender roles. Are people of a specific gender expected to give up a career once they have children? Can they continue working and raise their children at the same time? Or are they forced to give up the role of raising their children if they choose to continue with their career? Again, how do individual characters compare to the expectations?

RITUALS AND CEREMONIES

Each culture holds its own rituals and ceremonies around birth, which might be based on traditions, religion, economy, or science/magic levels. Such customs can take place before the birth (e.g., baby shower) or after the birth (e.g., baptism, circumcision, naming ceremonies). It is also possible that some cultural or religious traditions can be tied to historical science/magic levels since previously high mortality and illness rates might have encouraged practices like circumcision, quick blessings, or waiting to name a child in case they did not survive their first few days.

BIRTHDAYS

While some societies might consider all birthdays to be important, most hold at least one as an important event: coming of age, the day that marks the passage from childhood to adulthood. The specific transition age tends to vary from society to society and can be influenced by historical traditions, religions, legal systems, and more. Coming of age can be marked with a party or a special ceremony or ritual, and often denotes an increase in rights and responsibilities.

It is also possible that a society may not assign the coming of age to a specific birthday. Instead, the achievement might be characterized by an event, such as a first hunt, battle, or kill; first kiss; or first sexual experience. The milestone would generally depend on what a society considers important and how it defines an adult.

Other birthdays may be considered important within a society or to individuals. To some, certain birthdays mark new eras in a person's life. For others, every birthday is celebrated. Whatever the case, the custom needs to make sense to the society and the individuals living within it.

What do children and childhood mean to your story? Are children rare and something to be celebrated? Or are they a burden, considered just another mouth to feed?

TIDBIT 14

CHILDREN

What do children and childhood mean to your story? Are children rare and something to be celebrated? Or are they a burden, considered just another mouth to feed?

Children often mean various things to different cultures, especially in stories. Sometimes the importance of children, or lack thereof, is integral to a story's plot and a driving force for the characters' actions. More often, though, the value a society places on children contributes only a background influence within the story that provides a reason for a particular character's childhood, situation, or beliefs.

CHILDREN IN SOCIETY

Many factors can affect the importance of children within a society: from fertility rates and population levels to the types and availability of resources, technology, or magic. Cultural beliefs, especially those centered around gender norms, also drive the way children are viewed. Other factors that can influence the society's views of children include its state of affairs (peaceful, at war, struggling economically) and the number of orphans.

Children can also mean different things throughout a social hierarchy for much the same reasons. The affluent may have access to more resources and higher levels of technology or magic, providing them the means to indulge children and limit unwanted pregnancies. The poor, on the other hand, may view children in general as a combination of extra mouths to feed and additional hands for work.

Additionally, if the community of those wishing to marry is small, procreation may be a challenge and lead to each child being treasured.

None of these scenarios, of course, diminish the love often felt among families. Instead, they provide insight into the larger picture of a society, how individuals are raised, and how they feel toward having children of their own.

CHILDREN IN CHILDREN'S LITERATURE

Children play an important role in children's literature that typically is not found in other genres. This may seem obvious since children are the intended readers. However, when you write children's literature, you need to dive into the experiences of children in ways that most other types of literature do not.

Children are often the protagonists of children's books, even if the stories are not written from the protagonists' point of view. In children's literature, it is important for readers to see characters like themselves make decisions and drive the story, even if the narrative is told through the eyes of an adult. The children within the story also need personalities and backstories that make sense for their characters and help child readers connect with them, even when the readers do not have the same background.

This importance of children within the story is just as true for young adult fiction as it is for young-readers or middle-grade fiction. Even if the intended readership comes to these stories for escape, seeing people their own age make decisions that matter can help strengthen their own self-confidence.

CHILDREN IN APOCALYPTIC/POSTAPOCALYPTIC LITERATURE

Children can have a special meaning in apocalyptic and postapocalyptic literature. Children tend to be equated with hope, specifically for the survival of the species or society, but also in a general sense. Even the bleakest-looking postapocalyptic world can shine with hope if people have children who are thriving. Alternatively, a society that seems to be doing well does not have much hope if its birth rates are low and its children are dying.

Children can be a driving factor in this kind of literature. An illness may affect children more than adults (or vice versa) and the characters need to find out why. Perhaps the characters are driven to do something out of the ordinary to protect their children. Characters might even appear to act against their own nature in hopes of protecting their children—the innocent who are unable to protect themselves but offer hope in a time of darkness.

CHILDREN IN ROMANCE

In the romance genre, children and their importance can appear for a variety of reasons. Whether a main character desires children can be a driving force that shapes the type of relationship they seek. If one or more characters already have children, how other people act toward their children will affect the relationship they hold with those people.

Outside these arenas, children may appear as siblings or other family members of the main characters. As supporting characters, children can be integral to shaping the personality and opinions of the main characters. Positive interactions with children can also provide opportunities for less likeable characters to redeem themselves.

CHILDREN IN SPECULATIVE FICTION

In speculative fiction, especially those stories set in worlds other than modern-day Earth, children provide a great opportunity to explore another parameter of your world. For science-heavy worlds, what technologies do children grow up with? How has science affected birth rates and the health of children, or even the creation of children? Does the environment or society require that any particular surgeries be performed on or medicines be given to children?

In a fantasy setting, would children grow up around magic? If so, what kinds? How and when would they first be exposed to it? Would they themselves possess magic, or would they only be able to learn it after a certain age? Does magic affect birth rates and illnesses? If so, how?

CHILDREN IN STORIES

No matter what genre you write, it is important that you portray children accurately according to their age. For example, young children who speak with a more advanced vocabulary or act more mature than their age suggests can come across as jarring to a reader.

The exception to this may come from a world or character trait that affects the mental or emotional maturity rates of one or more children. If you include such an exception, do so purposely and explain it within the story. An example of this exception is Artemis Fowl in the series of the same name by Eoin Colfer. Artemis Fowl is a boy genius, and this is referenced frequently throughout the series to explain his intelligence, emotional distance, and general dislike for "childish" activities and behaviors.

CHILDHOOD AS BACKSTORY

With few exceptions, all characters once were (or are) children. When you know how children are generally viewed and treated in your world, you can delve deeper into the childhood of individual characters and determine how their childhood shaped their personality. What a character thinks of themselves, how they treat others, their approach to change and new things—all of these can probably be traced back to childhood experiences, joyous or traumatic.

What forms of recreation are available in
your world? What do your characters like to
do to relax? Tension may drive a story, but
looking forward to fun can drive a character.

TIDBIT 15

RECREATION

What forms of recreation are available in your world? What do your characters like to do to relax? Tension may drive a story, but looking forward to fun can drive a character.

Tension is the driving force behind any story, but it cannot make up the whole of your characters' lives, and certainly not the whole of your story's world. It is human nature, at least, to require regular rest and relaxation to prevent mental and physical degradation. For this reason, make sure you know what forms of recreation are available in your world and, specifically, what your characters like to do to relax and have fun.

SPORTS AND OTHER ATHLETICS

Most cultures have some kind of sports or other athletic activities that allow children or adults who participate to relax or have fun. These can range from athletics pertaining only to the body (e.g., running and hiking), ball sports (e.g., soccer and baseball), athletics requiring other kinds of tools (e.g., weight lifting and pole vaulting), or sports that require other creatures (e.g., polo and horseback racing). They may be something a person engages in alone, like jogging, or a team sport, like basketball.

The particular form of a sport can be determined as much by a society's environment as anything else. People who live near the ocean or a lake may prefer swimming, while people who live near mountains or caves may enjoy rock climbing or spelunking. Those who live in the forest may create tree-based sports, while a desert-based society may favor mounted sports.

Many sports offer entertainment for viewers as much as the participants. Whether a local sports match or an international tournament, athletic activities can broaden the range of entertainment available to your characters.

GAMES

Those who do not want to watch or take part in a sports match may relax by playing a game. Like sports, games range from those requiring no tools (e.g., guessing games) to having a complicated setup (e.g., tabletop gaming) and can be played by one person (e.g., solitary card games) or many (e.g., party games). Some games are based mostly on luck and strategy (e.g., poker), while others are games of skill (e.g., chess) or knowledge (e.g., trivia).

If your story takes place in modern or more scientifically advanced societies, video games and virtual reality open up another realm of possibility for recreation. Whether handheld, console, or virtual, such games can be played by one person or as part of an online community. Depending on the level of technology, virtual reality might also provide physical activity and travel without leaving a small area.

ART

Some people prefer to relax through a creative or cultural experience, such as the arts provide. Arts range from the literary and visual to the musical and tactile. Some participants seek a resulting product, while others pursue an experience or performance. Like sports, art provides recreation for those who create it and those who enjoy the results.

People explore the arts for various reasons. Some create art simply to deal with their own emotions, while others take it up professionally for others to enjoy. If any of your characters engage in art, I encourage you to dive into their reasons so you can better present the character to the reader.

TRAVEL AND EXPLORATION

Rather than stay in one place, some people prefer to explore locales they have never visited. Depending on the world you are writing, travel can be limited or, alternatively, a requirement of how your characters live. If they travel, explore their means of transportation. Do they walk, ride animals, teleport, or use mechanical vehicles, such as cars, aircraft, or ships? What types of activities do they partake in while exploring these new locales? Do they eat the local cuisine, shop, or learn about the local history and culture?

RECREATIONAL SUBSTANCES

Recreation can also include recreational substances, such as alcohol, drugs, or magic and technology that create similar effects. Such substances can be used to escape reality, calm down, or get an energy boost. Recreational substances may also be required to perform specific activities, like speaking with spirits or connecting with certain technologies.

If such substances are used within the world of your story, consider that individuals may be affected by them in different ways and what that means for the characters who use them. Also consider that such substances are often addictive and how that may appear throughout the world of your story.

UNIQUE FORMS OF RECREATION

If you are writing about a society beyond those here on Earth, do not be afraid to create new forms of recreation. Explore what is unique to the society you are writing about and how that has been modified for relaxation and fun. Basing recreation on a particular technology, magic, or tradition can deepen your world while providing a way to tie that form of recreation into the story.

BASIC LIFE ACTIVITIES

Sometimes all a character wants is the basics of rest: food, sleep, sex, or just a chance to stop worrying. As writers, we can put our characters through a lot, to the point where the dream of hot, tasty food or a soft, warm bed can keep them going just a little further. Keep in mind, though, that everyone has limits. If you push your characters too far, they may be forced to take breaks whether they want to or not, or you risk them reading as implausible.

INTROVERTS VERSUS EXTROVERTS

In addition to the forms of recreation available to them, consider whether your characters prefer to take part in social gatherings or be alone when you explore what your characters like to do for fun. Many people enjoy both, but some people relax and recharge better in one setting than the other. You will want to keep your characters' particular personalities in mind when delving into what they like to do and whether they need to recover from their fun experiences.

How is death treated in the world of your story? Is each death mourned, or is it so commonplace that people are indifferent? Are there funerals, songs, or wakes to honor the dead?

TIDBIT 16

DEATH

How is death treated in the world of your story? Is each death mourned, or is it so commonplace that people are indifferent? Are there funerals, songs, or wakes to honor the dead?

The view and treatment of death varies between cultures. To some, death is the ultimate ending; to others, it is simply the next step, with either an afterlife or incarnation to follow. Death is marked socially with different ceremonies and traditions. Similarly, the way you, as an author, approach death in your stories should vary from world to world and, within them, from culture to culture.

SOCIAL SIDE OF DEATH

Each culture treats their dead uniquely. Some bury the bodies in boxes (from simple to extremely elaborate) above or below ground. Some hold ceremonial pyres, sending those who have passed on into the afterlife in a blaze of fire and honoring their life as they do. The dead may be embalmed to preserve the body's form for travel into the afterlife. Alternatively, they may be cremated because there is no space to keep the body, the body is simply seen as a shell, or the body holds an illness that requires its destruction. For those who live at sea, the dead can be weighed down and dropped into its depths, while those who live in space might launch them into the void.

The treatments of remains can come from different aspects of a culture. Some originate in religion, which directs beliefs about the soul and what happens to people after death. Some treatments arise from a culture's environment. Still others are driven by sociopolitical issues, such as war or illness.

Beyond the treatment of the bodies, death is often marked socially with funerals or wakes to honor the life of the deceased. The people closest to the deceased, especially immediate family, may partake of a mourning period of a certain length because of their own grief or a socially imposed time period. Other customs include the creation of memento mori from the deceased's hair or the wearing of a specific color, like black or white.

In writing, the way death is viewed by characters and treated by their larger society can be tied to a larger piece of the story (war and illness or magical and scientific progress). On the other hand, you may need to dive into it further separately from any major story arcs or themes, if only to add emotional depth to your characters and their society. (For example, is death feared or welcomed by individual characters and why?)

SPIRITUAL SIDE OF DEATH

As an author, you can take the exploration of death a step beyond the views and customs of the societies and characters you write about. While we cannot be certain what happens after death in the real world, you can determine the truth for the specific worlds you create. Whether this takes the form of a heaven and hell, a deity of death who reaps souls, a cycle of incarnation, wandering spirits, some combination thereof, or beyond, you can define both the spiritual truths of death and the societal traditions around it.

COMBINING THE SOCIAL AND THE SPIRITUAL

Of course, your world's spiritual truths and society's customs may not be distinct from each other. Many stories dive into these individually and work to merge them through living characters interacting with the dead and the divine. This can take the form of ghost sightings, resurrection of the dead (or a perversion of it), spiritual guardians, or mediums and seers.

This idea can be taken a step further, in the form of creatures (or people) who cross the barrier between life and death or who defy death. Vampires, zombies, and mummies have appeared throughout literary and theatrical media, filling our minds with possibilities. Even in ancient cultures, the idea of evading or returning from death is evident in tales such as Achilles's invulnerability (except for the one spot on his heel) and Orpheus's journey into the underworld (he went to Hades to bring his wife back from the underworld, but in the last moment, he broke Hades's single condition and lost her).

BEYOND THE FACTS OF DEATH

When considering how death is treated and portrayed in a story, do not be afraid to explore beyond the facts. Dive into the emotions tied to it. Death can be viewed by cultures as both ugly and beautiful. This is especially visible in how death is portrayed in the arts. Explore what kinds of art your societies tie to death (visual art, music, writing, fashion, etc.). Do not arbitrarily assign arts, but delve into why each is connected to death.

Beyond emotion and art, how does death affect the people left behind? Grief is a real, solid emotion that can last for years, but those who remain can also be affected economically, politically, or religiously. Not all aspects will necessarily be portrayed explicitly in a story, but your knowledge of them can help you shape the way your characters face death, directly or otherwise.

EXAMPLES OF DEATH IN STORIES

Consider a land so embroiled in war or sickness that death is an everyday occurrence. Bodies are either buried in mass graves or burned en masse for lack of time, space, or general societal consideration, and personal mourning is lost in the larger emotional morass.

Consider a technically advanced society that has learned to conquer death, though at a cost that only the rich and powerful can pay. Death becomes a mark of squalor and a tool the rich wield to control the masses. (The book *Altered Carbon*, and the television show based on it, portray this concept well.)

In my own Evon series, the country has been at war for so long, there is no time for individual mourning. In response, the people have created a song to mourn those who are lost. In the desert, nomads burn the dead on pyres, while a society in the mountains uses Earth Magic to encase their dead in the solid rock of the mountains themselves.

PART VI

INTELLECTUAL ASPECTS

What level of technology or magic does
your world have? How does this translate
into things like housing, transportation,
food, and day-to-day life?

TIDBIT 17

TECHNOLOGICAL/MAGICAL ADVANCEMENT

What level of technology or magic does your world have? How does this translate into things like housing, transportation, food, and day-to-day life?

After you decide whether your world is based in science or magic (or both), the scope of the magic or technology within your societies comes into question. If you are writing your story in a historical or modern era, much of this can be based on what you see in daily life or research into the past. However, for those writing in futuristic Earth or other worlds, this question becomes important as the answers can help you better portray the daily life of your characters.

HOUSING

Housing is an interesting, and sometimes difficult, topic to think about. In many cases, environment and climate are as much a factor in determining a society's housing options as technology or magic levels. While the level of available technology or magic guides the complexity of the housing constructed, the environment may limit the resources for such construction. For example, a barren landscape may not provide trees for wood, and a grassy plain with a thick soil layer can complicate or inhibit stone harvesting. Climate helps determine the type of housing required (e.g., frequent flooding might require housing to be built on stilts or on higher ground).

However, advanced levels of technology or magic can improve the quality of housing and even increase the availability of resources by expanding the transportation of goods. Increased technology or magic levels might also provide additional resources as new materials are created rather than discovered and enhance security as energy/magic is manipulated into forms of protection (e.g., force fields or magical wards).

TRANSPORTATION

Types of transportation can be good indicators of technology or magic levels. The evolution of transportation often parallels the evolution of technology: from the domestication of horses and other beasts of burden, through the creation of carts and carriages, to the development of fuel-powered cars and spaceships. Similarly, magical forms of transportation can provide signs of different levels of magic, whether that comes in the form of flying brooms or carpets, the ability to transport instantly from one place to another, the "domestication" of more exotic creatures (e.g., dragons), or magical flight.

Also consider that forms of transportation affect not only the travel of individuals but also the transportation of goods. As transportation evolves, the availability of goods in one area becomes more widespread as quicker and farther-reaching transportation allows greater access in less time.

SUSTENANCE

As technology and magic evolve, so does the production and availability of food and water. Progression between levels can mean the difference between a hunter/gatherer society and the creation of farms and ranches to raise edible plants and animals. The evolution of irrigation and plumbing systems increases the accessibility of water and eases its transportation, which allows farmers to tend larger plots of land and society in general to expand farther away from major water sources. Faster and farther-reaching transportation opens access to nonnative food sources, increasing the variety in people's diets. And higher levels of technology and magic can even increase the availability of local food and water, due to increased fertility of the land, the introduction of techniques to better process previously inedible plants or animals, or the development of methods to cleanse or desalinate water.

Another aspect to consider when exploring the effect of technology/magic levels on sustenance is their effect on the economy. An increase in food and water sources supports more farmers and merchants. Increased technology or magic may lead to new occupations or novel applications of existing ones, opening up more jobs. Greater access to food and water can increase population levels, even as the population spreads out from its sources of food and water. These and other features of evolving technology and magic can greatly affect the formation of your world's societies and the lives of the characters you create.

COMMUNICATION

As the levels of technology and magic increase, so does the ease of communication. The exchange of information has evolved from solely face-to-face interactions to written forms of communication (stone tablets, parchment, papyrus, paper, books). Eventually, with the introduction of electricity, communication began to evolve further: from the telegraph to the telephone, from radio to television, from fax machines to email and text messengers, and on to video conferencing.

If you are writing stories based in a more technologically advanced world, these communication methods may be further evolved, possibly with holograms or mind-to-mind communication. If you are writing in a magic-based world, the evolution of communication may take a more magical form, such as telepathy, communication with plants or animals, communicating via the elements, and more.

WEAPONRY AND WARFARE

As technology and magic evolve, so do weapons and warfare. Weapons available to your characters may range from the simplistic (e.g., clubs, spears, and knives) to the most complex available based on current technology (e.g., guns, bombs, lasers, spells, potions, and poisons). When contemplating weaponry, consider the types of materials available to the society—including metals, crystals, or explosive elements—and the kinds of technical knowledge they possess related to the creation of weaponry. Such knowledge could relate to metal treatment, different complex mechanisms, or the application of electricity or magic.

Forms of warfare can be based on the weapons available (considering both the weapons' precision and accuracy and their capacity for destruction), the cultures of the societies that are fighting, and the terrain and climate.

HEALTH AND WELL-BEING

Increased levels of technology and magic often mean better health and well-being for a society overall. Improved access to medical care, whether science-, herb-, or magic-based, can increase chances of survival from illnesses, injuries, and childbirth and improve the general quality of life and longevity of the population.

OTHER PARTS OF DAILY LIFE

What other parts of daily life are affected by the levels of technology or magic present in your world? Are products handcrafted and, therefore, expensive and rare, or are they mass produced, making them cheaper and easier to obtain? What forms of entertainment are available because of technology or magic? Is there something unique to your world's levels of technology or magic that affects specific areas of characters' lives?

DISPARITY WITHIN SOCIETY

Most societies contain instances of inequality in living

standards. Depending on the social hierarchy, there will be many people who do not have access to the highest levels of technology or magic. Whether this is because of economic, sociopolitical, or some other disparity, you will need to determine who has access to which available technologies or magic and how it affects the lives of specific individuals within your story.

Be cognizant of your characters' language.
Time period, culture, and education can all
affect the language used.

TIDBIT 18

LANGUAGE

Be cognizant of your characters' language. Time period, culture, and education can all affect the language used.

Language is constantly evolving. Older generations and traditionalists often complain about this, as new words are accepted into the dictionary because of their wide use. *Irregardless* is the latest scandal I can think of, as several dictionaries have recognized and included it in their listings, if only as a nonstandard word used specifically in certain dialects.

Beyond scandals and the complaints of language purists, however, this evolution is important to consider when writing. Whatever your story's time period or location, there are always going to be words that are more appropriate for the characters to speak (and the narrative to include) and others that may best be avoided.

TIME-BASED LANGUAGE

Time is a powerful force, with regards to language as much as to stories. Even for those stories not based on Earth, a certain sense of time period is present in the stories you write, which can help you determine what kind of language to use.

For those stories written in modern-day settings, avoid words deemed antiquated, unless you are specifically aiming for a character to sound anachronistic. Some dictionaries mark whether a word—or a specific definition of it—is considered archaic. Even words like *amongst* and *amidst* (versus *among* and *amid*) are regarded as archaic and should be reviewed carefully to determine if they fit the story.

For stories set in older time periods, pay attention to when words were first introduced into the language. This may seem tedious, but consider, for example, the language we use today to speak of gender and sexual identity. Many of these words, like *gay* or *lesbian*, either did not exist in past centuries or had entirely different meanings.

LOCATION-BASED LANGUAGE

Location is also important when it comes to choosing language. Whether you look at the difference in dialect between countries (American English versus British, Australian, or Canadian English) or between different states or provinces, it is the details that will speak to your readers.

This is true for both dialogue and narrative, though dialogue is often more forgiving than narrative when it comes to the use of localized language. Localized slang and informal speech can be used in dialogue to portray a character's origin, while such language is generally discouraged in the larger narrative. Characters' accents, too, can be portrayed through dialogue via specific word choices or dialectal spellings (e.g., dropping the *g* from *-ing* endings: *goin'*, *makin'*, *seein'*, etc.).

When looking specifically at the narrative, you want to keep your audience in mind. There is a reason why some books may be "translated" when they are published in a different English-speaking country than their country of origin. Editors are trained to prefer a specific country's English. For example, an American editor will favor words like *cookies, fries,* and *chips* over their British equivalents, *biscuits, chips,* and *crisps,* as well as American spellings over British spellings, such as *license* versus *licence.*

However, translation between English-speaking countries may not be required and can even be detrimental to the story. Children's and young adult literature, like Eoin Colfer's *The Fowl Twins,* may require some changes between dialects to prevent confusion among younger audiences. Literature for older audiences, though—like the historical fantasy *His Majesty's Dragon* by Naomi Novik (originally published in the United Kingdom as *Temeraire*)— might lose the entire tone of the book if a modification of language were attempted.

In the end, the balance between being true to your story's location and writing to your audience lies in the understanding of your readers. Words like *blimey* (exclamation of amazement or surprise), *mate* (friend), and *car park* (parking lot or parking garage) may not be widely used or accepted in American

English, but their use is not going to be as confusing as, say, the use of *boot* (the trunk of a car) or *braces* (suspenders that hold up pants). However, when the word is the same but spelled slightly differently (e.g., *defense* versus *defence* or *color* versus *colour*), it is best to stick with the spelling specific to the book's country of publication.

EDUCATION-BASED LANGUAGE

However you look at it, language is learned, and that is as true for your characters as it is for you as a writer. Make sure individual characters speak words that match who they are and what they know. For example, a character would not speak of a "convocation" of eagles if they have no reason to know that the word refers to a group of eagles.

When choosing the level of language for your narrative, consider who your audience is and who is telling the story. If you are writing a children's book, you want to make sure the language used falls within your target reading level. When writing for adults, you can use more complex language that better fits the narrator. If you are writing in first person or third person limited, the narrative language should fit the point-of-view character, though perhaps more formal than they would speak in dialogue. For a more universal narrative, find the voice and tone that best match you, your style, and the story you are writing.

CULTURE-BASED LANGUAGE

Pay attention to the culture that prevails where your characters grow up and live, as there can be language rules specific to that culture. Certain words used frequently in everyday speech may identify a character as a member of that community. There may be words that are considered sacred, such as the name of a deity, and are used only in certain circumstances or by certain people.

A specific category of culture-based language is curse words. Depending on the intended audience, curses known in English today may not be acceptable in your story. To utilize swearing without introducing mainstream curse words into their stories, many authors create curse words specific to the cultures they develop. Authors who have done this to great effect are Eoin Colfer (*Artemis Fowl*) and James Dashner (*The Maze Runner*).

SLANG

Slang is language specific to a group of people, a time, a location, or an education level. Most of the time, slang words are not generally accepted as part of the mother language, though continued and widespread use may get them added to the language. For example, consider the word *okay*. It is generally accepted that *okay*, or *OK*, comes from *oll korrect*, a humorous spelling of *all correct*, and actually began as a joke. It was picked up by presidential campaigns for the 1840 US presidential election, which helped it gain the widespread popularity it has today.

Most of the time, slang in writing should be restricted to dialogue only, unless its use fits the narrator. Since slang is generally regarded as informal, consider its use in the narrative carefully. As for its use in dialogue, if the slang fits the speaker and the situation, then the only concern is whether it is understandable to your reader.

What shape does education take in your story?
Is it formal, or does it take place on the streets?
Is it provided for everyone or only for the elite?

TIDBIT 19

EDUCATION

What shape does education take in your story? Is it formal, or does it take place on the streets? Is it provided for everyone or only for the elite?

Whatever form it takes, education is important to every society. It encompasses how people learn to live, communicate, relate to others, and eventually make a living and support their community. Education fills most people's childhoods and can often extend well into their adult years.

LEARNING HOW TO LIVE

As humans, we spend our formative years constantly learning: to play, to communicate, to care for ourselves and others. In many societies, this kind of learning is not formal or structured. Instead, such things are often picked up by children in their daily interactions with their parents, their siblings, and others outside the family, as well as their general environment—natural, technological, magical, or otherwise.

Because such learning occurs almost automatically, it is interesting to consider how this informal and unstructured process would affect or be influenced by unusual circumstances. Many stories exist based on the idea of babes raised either by animals or in a society other than their birth culture (e.g., Tarzan or Romulus and Remus).

When writing speculative fiction, especially stories that feature nonhuman sentient species, consider that the human approach to learning and growth is not the only way. Some sentient species you write about may be born with instinctual or hereditary knowledge, making many of the initial life lessons humans must learn unnecessary.

TEACHING WHAT IS IMPORTANT

Once the initial life lessons have been learned, education often becomes more formal and potentially more varied. At this point, most societies only teach children what the society views to be important. Oftentimes, this is influenced by gender, economic or sociopolitical status, or religion.

The method of formal education can take many forms. In its simplest, education might be taken up by the child's family. More affluent families can hire tutors or nannies to educate their children. Some societies prefer to educate their children in a larger, more institutionalized format, such as boarding schools or day schools that may be funded privately or publicly. This societal preference may be taken a step further, requiring children to receive a certain level of education, whether provided by the family or public/private schools.

For those societies that do not require a certain level of education or offer public schooling, children may get their education from experience on the streets or among gangs. These children would learn important lessons based on what they need to survive rather than whether their actions are on the right or wrong side of the law.

TRAINING FOR THE JOB

After learning what society deems important, children—and in some cases, adults—must then begin the process of learning a trade. In some societies or communities within them, this process may be initiated by or integrated into formal education. This could include family trades, in which families take full responsibility for their children's education and may combine basic and trade-specific education.

For those societies that separate basic and trade-specific education, the latter can be offered in many ways. Some societies have colleges, universities, or trade schools geared toward specific areas of expertise. Other societies may expect people of a certain age to apprentice under a master of their preferred trade and learn either directly from the master or in a school-like setting under the master's journeymen.

One thing to consider for any job training is how the education costs are paid. Institutions can have high tuitions, which may require students' families to save money over several years or obligate students to pay off a debt throughout their adulthood (either to a bank or a benefactor). Tuition may also be paid through scholarships offered by the state, private parties, or the institutions themselves.

Even children who apprentice under a master would most likely have to pay for their education in some manner. Payment may be money or trade items provided by the family, or it could take the form of a debt to the master, to be paid off over time through some form of tender or amount of work performed under the master's name.

If a person's chosen trade requires them to work for another person's business (rather than working for themselves), the employer may provide its own job-specific training. Generally, this ensures the quality and type of work produced matches a standard set for that specific business.

Oftentimes, training for a trade does not end. Newly created techniques, discoveries, and other information are frequently shared within a trade's communities. To assure they remain productive and profitable, individuals within these communities would need to keep up with the latest trends and advancements.

CHANGING COURSE

Sometimes, a person selects a trade they do not enjoy, or they lose interest in the trade over time. While finding joy or interest in one's work may not matter in some societies, there are many societies that offer their citizens the chance to return to a learning environment and choose a new trade. There may even be people within a society who are always learning and moving from one trade to another as they seek the next venture to interest them.

Part VII

Artistic Aspects

The inclusion of art, such as dance, fashion, music, and literature, can help you explore your story and the cultures within it. What types of art do you depict in your story to expand your world?

TIDBIT 20

ART

The inclusion of art, such as dance, fashion, music, and literature, can help you explore your story and the cultures within it. What types of art do you depict in your story to expand your world?

All cultures have some form of art as a means of expressing emotion and creativity. Beautiful or ugly, art tends to stimulate one or more senses. It can be created for its own sake or as a feature of mundane products. Whether or not your story specifically features creative individuals, the portrayal of art can make your world feel more real and bring your reader deeper into the story.

THE PURPOSE OF ART

There are many purposes that can drive art, and even a single piece can be impelled by several. For most creators, the initial impulse behind their art is to release the emotions, stories, or ideas that fill them and demand to be turned into reality. Upon completion, artwork may be secreted away, perhaps due to the creator's fear of others' reactions or shame or dislike for the piece. Such emotions are often rooted in the creator's personal history or the expectations of the society in which they were raised.

Those creators who decide to take their art to the next level will most likely go through several revisions or versions, depending on the type of creation, before they deem a piece ready for public presentation. It is during the revision process that an artwork's other purposes generally come to light. The creator may wish to evoke emotions in others similar to those the creator experienced while producing the piece. Perhaps the creator wants to capture the story of a particular event and preserve it for others to understand. The artwork may serve a religious purpose, to portray a deity or an image that venerates a deity, or it may be used for sociopolitical or economic purposes, with the aim of convincing consumers of a particular idea. Or the piece may simply be a means to earn the creator wealth.

VISUAL AND TACTILE ARTS

In many cultures, the word *art* is tied specifically to visual and tactile arts. Paintings, drawings, sculptures, pottery, tapestries—these are often the first things that come to mind when people think of art. How do these translate into the world you are writing?

What materials are used to create drawings or sketches? Do artists use charcoal, ash, or another material, like graphite, to produce such images? What surfaces do they produce these creations on? If they create paintings, what do artists use for paints? Do they use natural colorants or chemically derived pigments to tint the paint? For pieces such as sculptures or pottery, what type of material are they fabricated from (e.g., metal, stone, wood, clay)? And for artistic textiles like tapestries, what creation methods (e.g., weaving, knitting, crocheting), materials (e.g., plant material like flax or animal material like wool), and dyes (colors and sources) are used to make them?

Music and Performance Arts

Unlike the final static product of most visual and tactile arts, music and performance arts embody movement and change. There are often two parts to music and performance arts: the initial creation and the performance.

The initial creation is the private portion of the art the consumer does not see. This includes composing music, piecing together lyrics, choreographing dances, and writing plays. These endeavors result in visual or written products that are interpreted by those who perform the eventual pieces. All these works go through their own revision processes before they are deemed ready to be presented to the public.

The performance portion presents these works as performances for audiences to listen to or watch. This is accomplished by musicians, singers, conductors, dancers, actors, and all the unseen behind-the-scenes creators. Similar to the initial creation portion, the performance portion requires revision—in this case, practice—before the performance is opened to the public.

LITERARY ARTS

For you as a writer, the literary arts may be the first form of art that comes to mind, but how often do you think to integrate written works into the world of your story? If you set your story in a world based on Earth, this can be easy, but make sure any existing literature you reference is already published and available during your story's time frame. If you create your own world, incorporating written material may be a little trickier.

Literary arts can range from fiction to nonfiction and take the form of treatises, novels, short stories, poetry, lyrics for music, prophecies, and riddles. They can be handwritten, typed, or spoken and bound in books, rolled into scrolls, or presented in electronic formats. Since the literary arts are often the most conducive for portraying a story, this is often how history is preserved, beyond the oral medium. And while oral storytelling is technically not literary, oral tradition is certainly the predecessor of the literary arts.

ART IN THE MUNDANE

Art does not have to be made in and of itself. It can have practical purposes, especially for works based on the mundane. In fact, many cultures find ways to turn the necessary and mundane into art. Food, architecture, interior design, fashion—all of these can be created to both serve their innate function (feed, shelter, and clothe) and evoke emotion, tell a story, or portray a certain idea. This type of art may not be restricted to a single iteration but produced again and again for many to enjoy. If you write about a nonhuman species, consider what else might act as art in the mundane. For example, some species communicate solely in song (e.g., whales and dolphins).

UNIQUE ART

Art does not have to be restricted to what our world has known or currently knows. If your stories are based in worlds other than modern Earth, they may include something unique that lends itself to a new type of art. There may be a technology or magic that allows creators to use thought or light as their medium. Perhaps magic enables artists to create out of the elements, or technology permits crafters to shape their creations at the molecular level.

One example of a form of art unique to the technology of a world is the holographic novel portrayed in several *Star Trek* series. Sometimes based on literary works or historical events, a holographic novel provides a realistic, interactive environment in which a story plays out. The person enjoying the piece can decide whether to watch the story without interacting or to take on the role of one or more characters within the story.

STANDALONE VERSUS INTERACTIVE

Not all art is meant to be enjoyed from a passive vantage point. Sometimes, art is created specifically for viewer or consumer interaction. Such forms of art are more common in our modern societies: choose-your-own-adventure books, interactive museum exhibits, video games, visual novels, and virtual-reality simulations. Consider how the technology or magic available in your world may lend itself to such pieces of art.

ARTS AND SOCIETY

Each society has its own relationship with and views of art, even throughout its own history. In some cases, certain forms of art are held in high regard. Their creators may be placed in a higher social tier or compensated well for their creations, either by the state, individual benefactors, companies, or the general public. Similarly, specific types of art might be created and upheld as the ideal, perhaps as a form of propaganda.

In other cases, certain forms of art are not considered valuable contributions to society but viewed more as hobbies or a waste of time that could be spent on more productive endeavors. In these cases, artists are more likely to feel shame about their work and conclude that their art has no meaning.

Beyond the dismissal of art is its suppression. This relationship with art is especially present in societies that hold one group of people more important or greater than another. Certain types of art and literature may be banned or burned. In such societies, creators may hide away their work to protect themselves or use their art to stand against the suppression and empower others.

PART VIII

JOURNEY'S END

What is the objective truth of your story's world? How does it differ from the understanding of the narrator and other characters? Why?

TIDBIT 21

OBJECTIVE VERSUS SUBJECTIVE TRUTH

**What is the objective truth of your
story's world? How does it differ from
the understanding of the narrator and
other characters? Why?**

Unlike journalists, historians, and memoirists, fiction
writers are capable of a uniquely privileged view of
the world they write about: the objective truth. A
fiction writer can understand exactly what happens in
their world and why, without the interpretation of
others or the filters of emotion, prejudice, or trauma
with which nonfiction writers must contend.

There are various reasons for characters to have
a different understanding of their world than what is
objectively true. For some, it is simply ignorance, but

depending on the world you write in, the difference could be caused by something much larger.

IMPORTANCE OF THE OBJECTIVE TRUTH

Much of the time, the objective truth is not something discussed within a story because most characters do not know that truth. Without using an outside narrator, weaving such information into the story can be difficult and sound forced.

Instead, the objective truth acts as a guide for the writer and provides motive and reasoning for characters and events. If you do not know the truth of what happens in your story and why the characters do what they do or react as they do, it is difficult to consistently portray events and characters' actions, even through the lens of the point-of-view character. Knowing the objective truth can also help you determine the best point of view for telling the story.

Identifying the objective truth can help you decide whether a prologue, an epilogue, or accompanying stories would be worthwhile. Prologues are not always popular with agents and acquisition editors;

however, a prologue or epilogue written from a point of view other than the one used for the main story is often the only way to convey certain information to readers—and establish greater curiosity within them. James Dashner does this well in his Maze Runner series, in which the epilogue of each book is a memo written by one of the people in charge of the larger program. Each epilogue provides a wider view of what is going on—and possibly a hint of how much more the characters have to deal with in the next book.

SPIRITUALITY VERSUS RELIGION

What exists beyond mortal life? While this is not something that can be answered in the real world, a fiction writer can define both the spiritual reality of their world and the way the mortal characters understand it. The writer can also determine why there may be a disparity between the two. Is no one capable of observing what lies beyond the mortal realm? Do deities take a hands-off approach toward their people, leading mortals to either lose faith or forget about them? Or have pretender gods or false prophets swooped in and spread lies that turn the people away from a truth they may have once known?

Whatever the differences or reasons, understanding the objective truth can, if nothing else, help a writer shape events such as divine interventions, blessings, and miracles, or the lack of them when they are expected. In more spiritually active books, deities may be characters that deal with the disparity between truth and religion.

HISTORY AS INTERPRETATION

There is a phrase attributed to Winston Churchill that speaks to the concept of history as an interpretation: "History is written by the victors." Except the phrase did not originate with Churchill and may not have even been spoken by him.

Whether or not you believe the phrase, history as people know it does not always match what actually occurred. The reasons for this can be as simple and innocent as written records being lost or misinterpreted over time. Or the explanations may be more sinister, as people in power manipulate records and beliefs so that certain things are forgotten or remembered a specific way.

An example of this idea is the Mandela effect—the phenomena of large groups of people remembering events or ideas that either did not exist or occurred somewhat differently than the people collectively remember. The supposed Churchill quote noted earlier is a perfect example of this. With this phenomenon, even recent history can be used to mislead characters—and through them, the reader.

CHARACTER INTERPRETATION

Characters can have various reasons for interpreting events differently than they occur. Sometimes, an event can trigger high emotions, obscuring details and enhancing others in a character's memory. Perhaps a traumatic response interferes with how someone experiences an event, overlapping a past event over the current one and adding an extra layer of confusion. Or maybe the way a character experiences the world in general (perhaps due to injuries or atypical mental processes) provides a view of the event that does not appear to match the objective truth.

An example of character interpretation common in fiction is the unreliable narrator. Any of the previously stated reasons—or even intentional misleading on the part of the narrator—can lead the reader to understand the story and world in a way that does not match reality.

IGNORANCE

Sometimes, the difference between a character's understanding and the objective truth is simply ignorance. While not always the case, this reasoning is especially useful when the main character is a student. The story may begin with the character knowing nothing—or at most, only the basics—of the world being introduced. As the story progresses, the character slowly learns more of the truth, which the reader learns as well.

Sometimes, though, ignorance is not completely alleviated within a single story. You may know the truth of your world from the beginning, but it can take an entire series (if not more) for characters to learn the full truth of their world.

Conclusion

Next Step in the Journey

As you step past the twenty-first signpost, take some time to rest and sit with what you have learned, both about worldbuilding and about your own stories. Each tidbit, though brief, encourages a deeper dive into broad aspects of the worlds you write, a journey that can be as overwhelming as it is thought-provoking.

X Marks the Spot

When we began this adventure together, I explained the treasure we sought: better and truthful understanding of the worlds you write. The tidbits presented within this volume are meant to provide you with steps toward that understanding, but it is rarely a task that can be completed in a single journey. As I have seen proven in the worldbuilding classes I teach, your current projects, and your progress within each one, will influence which tidbits speak to you when you open this book.

Once you have familiarized yourself with the twenty-one signposts, choose a world you are writing and revisit the road map. Whether you are just beginning to form the world or you are figuring out the last missing details, focusing on a particular world as you follow the map will help trigger more specific details along the way.

JOURNEY NOT ALONE

As writers, many of us feel like solitary creatures, sitting alone to handwrite, type, or dictate the stories in our heads. But however long we spend thinking about our worlds, there is something powerful about discussing them with trusted companions. Sometimes a single hour of conversation can uncover more than days of writing ever will. If you do not have someone to discuss worlds and stories with, reach out to local or online writing groups. Seek out critique groups that fit your writing style and genres or find a developmental editor, like me, who can work with you to uncover more about your worlds and ferret out any missing pieces in your stories.

For me, the process of writing this book was filled with many people. Long before this book was ever proposed, the ideas within it evolved through reading, writing, and conversations with both writers and nonwriters. When I created my original world-building class, a conversation with my father led me to the acronym PERSIAN, which has provided me a teaching structure ever since. My first worldbuilding classes were hosted by the Houston Writers Guild and Inklings Publishing, and later by Creative Central and Debbie Burns in Fiction Expedition. Every class I taught brought up new aspects to consider in world-building, as attendees applied what they learned to their worlds.

With the encouragement of Debbie Burns and my fellow press owner, Ynes Freeman, I drew from the knowledge that informed my worldbuilding classes and developed posts that were shared in Creative Central. This eventually evolved into the daily tips I post to my editing social media pages under #EditingTidbit. Comments by others on these posts helped me refine the wording of the individual tidbits and expand them into longer discussions that eventually informed this book.

More helpful than the comments on these posts were the participants of Word Splurge, a writing program run by Balance of Seven. Our weekly Tod's Thoughts—group developmental editing sessions led by me—touched on many a writing topic that helped me understand what other writers found most beneficial for worldbuilding and developing other areas of their stories.

Finally, the compilation of this book, and the rest of the Fiction Tinker's Guide series, was prompted by Ynes Freeman. Her presence and determination helped me finalize this book when I had struggled over not finishing a book for several years. Holla Watson, whose beautiful artwork adorns this entire volume, was sweet enough to let me call her anytime to discuss how to break down some of the tidbits in this book. Charleigh Brennan, fellow specfic author and gamer, generously acted as beta reader, providing insights on tone that I greatly appreciate. And Kathy Riggs Larsen, long-time nonfiction editor, ran through this book with a fine-tooth comb, pointing out what was confusing or needed rearranging and allowing me to debate with her all along the way. Between these four lovely women, I received the help I needed to organize my thoughts, refine my wording, and realize what I may be forgetting.

RESOURCES

TIDBIT 1: LAW OF THE LAND

Crawford, Jeremy. *Dungeons & Dragons Player's Handbook.* Renton, WA: Wizards of the Coast LLC, 2014.

Pierce, Tamora. *Sandry's Book.* Circle of Magic. New York: Scholastic, 1997.

TIDBIT 2: NATURE

"Jack and the Beanstalk." *Wikipedia.* Updated January 10, 2021, 17:43. https://en.wikipedia.org/wiki/Jack_and_the_Beanstalk.

Roddenberry, Gene. *Star Trek: The Original Series.* Directed by Marc Daniels, Joseph Pevney, et al. Aired 1966–1969, on NBC. https://www.netflix.com/title/70136140.

TIDBIT 3: NONHUMANS

Tinker, Dorothy. *Lost King.* 2nd ed. Evon. Dallas: Balance of Seven, 2018.

Resources

TIDBIT 4: POLITICS

Dalberg-Acton, John, correspondent. Letter to Mandell
 Creighton. April 5, 1887. Archived by Online
 Library of Liberty. Accessed January 12, 2021.
 https://oll.libertyfund.org/page/acton-creighton-
 correspondence-1887.

TIDBIT 6: ECONOMY

Niccol, Andrew, dir. *In Time*. 2010; Los Angeles: New
 Regency Productions, 2011. https://www.amazon
 .com/Time-Justin-Timberlake/dp/B006PERRMY.

TIDBIT 10: FAMILY

Huxley, Aldous. *Brave New World*, 1st Perennial Classics
 ed. New York: HarperCollins, 1998.
Lowry, Lois. *The Giver*, Media Tie In ed. Boston: HMH
 Books for Young Readers, 1993.

TIDBIT 11: LOVE

GCT A. "The 8 Ancient Greek Words for Love." *Greek
 City Times*, February 14, 2020. https://greekcity
 times.com/2020/02/14/the-8-ancient-greek-words-
 for-love.

TIDBIT 12: MARRIAGE

Livingston, David, dir. *Star Trek: Enterprise*. Season 2, episode 14, "Stigma." Aired February 5, 2003, on UPN. https://www.netflix.com/title/70158332.

TIDBIT 13: BIRTH CULTURE

Huxley, Aldous. *Brave New World*, 1st Perennial Classics ed. New York: HarperCollins, 1998.

TIDBIT 14: CHILDREN

Colfer, Eoin. *Artemis Fowl*. New York: Hyperion Miramax, 2001.

TIDBIT 16: DEATH

Kalogridis, Laeta. *Altered Carbon*. TV series based on *Altered Carbon* by Richard K. Morgan. 2016; Vancouver, British Columbia: Netflix, 2018. https://www.netflix.com/title/80097140

Morgan, Richard K. *Altered Carbon*. New York: Random House, 2002.

Tinker, Dorothy. *Gift of War*, 2nd ed. Evon. Dallas: Balance of Seven, 2018.

———. *Peace of Evon*, 2nd ed. Evon. Dallas: Balance of Seven, 2017.

TIDBIT 18: LANGUAGE

Colfer, Eoin. *The Fowl Twins*. Los Angeles: Disney Hyperion, 2019.

Dashner, James. *The Maze Runner*. New York: Delacorte Press, 2009.

Francis, Jeffrey. "US vs. UK Editions of *The Fowl Twins*: Super In-Depth Comparison (Part 1)." *Artemis Fowl Confidential*, October 6, 2020. https://www.artemis-fowl.com/2020/10/06/us-vs-uk-editions-of-the-fowl-twins-super-in-depth-comparison-part-1.

Merriam-Webster. "Irregardless." *Merriam-Webster.com Dictionary*. Accessed January 12, 2021. https://www.merriam-webster.com/dictionary/irregardless.

Novik, Naomi. *His Majesty's Dragon*. New York: Del Rey, 2006.

TIDBIT 19: EDUCATION

Burroughs, Edgar Rice. *Tarzan of the Apes*. New York: A. L. Burt Company, 1914. Archived by Archive.org. Accessed January 12, 2021. https://archive.org/details/in.ernet.dli.2015.94628.

TIDBIT 20: ART

Berman, Rick, Michael Piller, and Jeri Taylor. *Star Trek: Voyager*. Directed by David Livingston, Winrich

Kolbe, Allan Kroeker, et al. Aired 1995–2001, on UPN. https://www.netflix.com/title/70158331.

Kroeker, Allan, dir. *Star Trek: Enterprise*. Season 4, episode 3, "These Are the Voyages . . . ." Aired May, 13, 2005, on UPN. https://www.netflix.com/watch/70177862.

Roddenberry, Gene. *Star Trek: The Next Generation*. Directed by Cliff Bole, Les Landau, Winrich Kolbe, et al. Aired 1987–1994, by Viacom. https://www.netflix.com/title/70158329.

TIDBIT 21: OBJECTIVE VERSUS SUBJECTIVE TRUTH

Dashner, James. *The Death Cure*. New York: Delacorte, 2011.

———. *The Maze Runner*. New York: Delacorte Press, 2009.

———. *The Scorch Trials*. New York: Delacorte, 2010.

Phelan, Matthew. "The History of 'History Is Written by the Victors.'" *Slate.com*, November 26, 2019. https://slate.com/culture/2019/11/history-is-written-by-the-victors-quote-origin.html.

CONCLUSION: NEXT STEP IN THE JOURNEY

Balance of Seven (website). https://www.balanceofseven.com.

Resources

Balance of Seven. "Word Splurge." Patreon. https://www.patreon.com/BalanceofSeven.

Brennan, Charleigh. "Charleigh Brennan Author." Facebook. https://www.facebook.com/charleighbrennanauthor.

———. "Fairy Godmother in Disguise." Patreon. https://www.patreon.com/fairygodmotherindisguise.

"Creative Central." Facebook. https://www.facebook.com/groups/creativecentral.

Debbie Burns (website). https://www.debbieburns.me.

Freeman, Ynes. "Ynes Malakova." Amazon.com. https://www.amazon.com/Ynes-Malakova/e/B07G2LYVXL.

Houston Writers Guild (website). https://www.houstonwritersguild.org.

Inklings Publishing (website). https://www.inklingspublishing.com.

Theodore Niretac Tinker (website). http://theodorentinker.com.

Tinker, Theodore Niretac. "TNT Editing." Facebook. https://www.facebook.com/TNTinkerEditing.

———. "TNT Editing." Twitter. https://twitter.com/TNTinkerEditing.

Watson, Holla. Sweet Issues Art (website). https://www.sweet-issues-art.com.

INDEX

Index

Index

clerics. *See* magic, classes
climate, 3, 18, 19, 20
   and housing, 138
   and warfare, 142
clothing
   as art, 162–63, 168
   and death, 131
   and economy, 49, 52
   and marriage, 100
   and religion, 57
cohabitation, 45
coins. *See* tender, legal
college, 158
colonization, 42–43, 45
coming of age, 110
commodities, as tender. *See*
   tender, legal
communication, 141–42
   as art, 168
   between mortals and
      spiritual beings, 11
companies
   hierarchy, 34
   politics, 34, 35, 37
competition, 44
conflict. *See* multicultural
   interactions; tension
con men, 54
conquest, 42–43

contemporary fiction, 2, 9,
   10, 137, 148
contraception. *See* pregnancy,
   prevention
cooperation. *See* alliance
copper. *See* tender, legal
corporations. *See* companies
corruption. *See under* politics
countries
   politics of, 33–34
   See also multicultural
      interactions
creation. *See* art
creatures
   magical, 10, 27
   mythical, 28, 29
   See also immortals;
      nonhumans
credits, as currency. *See*
   tender, legal
cremation, 130, 134
crime syndicate, 35
cultural appropriation, 12
culture
   and art. *See* art
   birth. *See* childbirth
   death. *See* death
   and education. *See*
      education

Index

Index

Index

Index

metals, precious. *See under* tender, legal

microorganisms, 28, 30
  See also bacteria; pollen; seeds; spores; virus

militia, 35

monarch, 32–33, 34

money. *See* economy

monotheism. *See* religion, types of

monsters, 28, 29

moon cycles, 16–17, 21, 22

morality, 37–38, 62

mortals
  and religion, 58–59, 174
  and spirituality, 11, 58–59, 174

mountains, 20, 122, 134

mourning, 128–29, 131, 134

multicultural interactions, 40–46
  alliance, 44, 46
  cohabitation, 45
  colonization, 42–43, 45
  competition, 44
  conquest, 42–43
  exceptions to the rules, 46
  integration, 45

multicultural interactions (*continued*)
  subjugation, 42–43
  symbiosis, 45
  trade, 41–42
  war. *See* war

mummies. *See* undead

music
  as art, 162–63, 166
  and death, 128–29, 134

mythical creatures. *See* creatures, mythical

myths and legends, 28, 74–75

natural disasters, 18

nature, 16–22
  as background, 17, 20
  beneficial vs. dangerous, 16–17, 21–22
  and clothing, 18
  and culture, 18–19
  and education, 156
  laws of, 9–15
  and magic, 14, 18, 22
  and recreation, 122
  retaliation of, 17
  and society, 18, 19
  of the soul. *See* souls
  as story element, 17, 18–19, 20

Index

Index

Index

ABOUT THE AUTHOR

Theodore Niretac Tinker is a worldbuilder. Words and worlds are his passion; quality and consistency, his goal. A three-time award-winning fantasy author, he has been through such a winding journey as an author that he wishes to help as many other writers and authors navigate the journey with ease and quality as possible.

With a certificate in editing from the University of Chicago (home of *The Chicago Manual of Style*), Tod has spent the last few years achieving this goal by providing editing services for his fellow writers. His bachelor's degree in mathematics gives him an eye for details, as well as the big picture, enhancing his worldbuilding skills.

About the Author

Tod supports his many literary endeavors with an endless supply of chocolate, which he hoards in his library alongside his books like any good dragon. You can follow Tod on Facebook and Twitter at @TNTinkerEditing for daily discussions under the hashtag #EditingTidbit.

Check out TheodoreNTinker.com for more information on Tod's editing services and available publications. Many of his previous fiction publications, including his Evon series and eleven short stories, can be found under his former pen name, Dorothy Tinker.

ABOUT THE ILLUSTRATOR

Holla Watson is a bipolar artist, teacher, creative energy healer, and illustrator who loves fantasy and whimsy. As a child, her whole world was vibrant with imagination and color. She collected odd, shiny, and silly things, using them to create art and make up stories. Her heart, body, and soul are consumed by art—her North Star during the traumatic challenges of her adolescence and early adulthood.

Her truth? Art saves lives.

When she's not helping others find their souls through art, you can find Holla video gaming, hiking, hanging with her animal family, and playing with her two kids. Come say hi at @Sweet.Issues_art on Instagram, @SweetIssuesArt on Facebook, and Sweet-Issues-Art.com.